W9-CWV-640

Overcoming Barriers to Witnessing

OVERCOMING BARRIERS TO WITNESSING

DELOS MILES

BROADMAN PRESS
Nashville, Tennessee

© Copyright 1984 ● Broadman Press
All Rights Reserved

4262-45

ISBN: 0-8054-6245-7
Dewey Decimal Classification: 248.5
Subject Heading: WITNESSING
Library of Congress Catalog Number: 83-70641

Printed in the United States of America

Library of Congress Cataloging in Publication Data

Miles, Delos.
    Overcoming barriers to witnessing.

    Bibliography: p.
    1. Witness bearing (Christianity)   I. Title.
BV4520.M55   1984   248'.5   83-70641
ISBN 0-8054-6245-7 (pbk.)

Dedicated to the memory of Harold B. Dunn,
a humble Christian layman
of Crewe, Virginia,
With whom I spent many hours
fishing for men.

Contents

Preface

1. The Fear Barrier.. 13
   Objection: "I'm afraid."

2. The Perfection Barrier.. 21
   Objection: "I'm not good enough."

3. The Spiritual Gift Barrier 29
   Objection: "I don't have the gift."

4. The Professional Barrier 39
   Objection: "That's a minister's work."

5. The Model Barrier 47
   Objection: "I'm no Billy Graham."

6. The Time Barrier 55
   Objection: "I don't have time."

7. The Knowledge Barrier.. 63
   Objection: "I don't know how."

8. The Power Barrier 77
   Objection: "I don't have the power to do that."

9. The Theological Barrier.. 87
   Objection: "I don't believe . . ."

10. The Stranger Barrier 99
    Objection: "You can't witness to total strangers."

11. The Age Barrier 111
    Objection: "I'm too old."

12. The Kinship-Friendship Barrier............................... 123
    Objection: "I'm too close."

Preface

Herein is a mystery: often it takes God longer to get a Christian ready to witness than it takes him to get a lost person ready to be saved. Some persons have not been saved because nobody has invited them to the King's banquet (see Matt. 22:1-14; Luke 14:12-24). Ask them and see.

This book is about breaking down barriers to witnessing which are mostly internal. Essentially I am seeking to answer the question: "How can we overcome those objections which Christians themselves raise against sharing their faith?"

Many have dealt with the external barriers to witnessing. A good bit has been written on overcoming excuses and objections which unbelievers give for not becoming Christians. I do not attempt to cover that territory again.

What I want to do here is to confront head-on those objections which Christians most often give for not actively and intentionally bearing witness to Jesus Christ among their lost loved ones, friends, neighbors, associates, acquaintances, and among total strangers. I have written these chapters primarily for lay Christians who are serious about overcoming those hindrances to witnessing which they recognize in themselves and in their fellow workers. The volume is also addressed to pastors and other church staff members who need a tool to help their congregation overcome the objections which they raise to the words of Jesus, "You shall be my witnesses . . . to the end of the earth" (Acts 1:8).

A. C. Archibald found five main factors in the conversion of any person: God, the Bible, the gospel in Christ, the Holy Spirit, and the agency of man. The first four of these he found always functioning in every attempt to win the lost. "They are more depend-

able than the stars," said he. But that last factor of human agency
he found uncertain.[1]

That fifth factor which Archibald called "the agency of man" is
my subject matter. Particularly am I concerned with the human
agent who labels himself or herself "Christian."

One WMU president gave three reasons for not witnessing:

- "I didn't think God intended for me to witness.'
- "I didn't know how."
- "I didn't think I had a testimony."

A 1969 comparative study of witnessers and nonwitnessers in
the Southern Baptist Convention revealed that the three top hindrances to witnessing were: (1) lack of dependence upon the Holy
Spirit; (2) lack of knowledge about witnessing; and, (3) personality
is not the type to do personal witnessing. Interestingly, both witnessers and nonwitnessers gave the same three hindrances, but in
different order. Nonwitnessers ordered their hindrances (2), (3),
and (1) respectively.[2]

An Episcopalian, Joyce Neville, says: "A dozen barriers prevent
Christians from talking about their faith."[3] Neville then proceeds
to list and briefly discuss ten of those twelve barriers. Although
these overlap to some extent with the hindrances and reasons
given above, we might be helped by comparing Neville's list with
the above and with the twelve which I treat.

The ten barriers to witnessing which Neville singles out are:

- Our lack of awareness of unexpected opportunities.
- Our lack of courage to witness.
- We do not want to threaten the status quo of our relationship
  with another.
- We don't know how to begin talking about spiritual matters.
- We feel that we may be implying that we are trying to tell
  other persons how to live their lives.
- It requires more knowledge and demands more time and
  involvement than we wish to give.
- Many Christians think that to witness verbally they must
  have an aggressive personality.

- Some think we must be a theologian or be able to quote Scripture abundantly.
- We may think we don't have anything in a spiritual way to give another.
- We think people are not interested in spiritual discussions.[4]

I believe the twelve barriers which I treat will touch on all sixteen of the above. It is my conviction that each generation of Christians is responsible for evangelizing the lost of that generation. The only lost persons whom we can effectively evangelize are those who are now alive or who will live during our lifetime.

Also, I am convinced that if we go to share our faith without knowing our faith, we may end up trying to share ignorance with ignorance. This is where Evangelism Explosion and other formal lay witness training can fill a vital role. Like C. H. Spurgeon I caution my students not to think in smoke or to preach in a cloud.

There is a wise carpenter's adage which says: "Measure twice and saw once." Some of us don't measure even once before we saw, let alone twice. One of my goals in this book is to get us Christians to measure twice and saw once. I want the passion of my life and yours to be fishing for men, but not promiscuously fishing for them.

Roger C. Palms, editor of *Decision* magazine, has told about seeing a notice posted along the Minnesota River which allowed short-term "promiscuous fishing." Believe it or not, the notice had been posted by the fish-and-wildlife authorities. A large number of carp were smothering due to low-water levels. People could spear, club, or catch fish without regard to the method used for several weeks. Apparently the authorities judged such promiscuous fishing to be better than allowing the fish to die of low-oxygen levels in the water. That promiscuous fishing resulted in large mounds of dead or dying fish being heaped up on the shore. What an ugly sight and an awful stench![5]

Think of that, "promiscuous fishing." God never posts notices like that. If we Christians do any promiscuous fishing for men, we shall do it illegally. We'll be breaking the law of love. In fishing for men, promiscuous fishing is never allowed. Clubs and spears are not permitted in the fine art of fishing for men.

Notes

1. Arthur C. Archibald, *New Testament Evangelism* (Philadelphia: Judson Press, 1946), pp. 109-111.

2. See "Reaching People: a Study of Witnessers and Nonwitnessers," RS-117, September 1969, an unpublished research project by the Research and Statistics Department of the Baptist Sunday School Board, SBC, Nashville, Tennessee.

3. Joyce Neville, *How to Share Your Faith Without Being Offensive* (New York: Seabury Press, 1979), p. 33.

4. Ibid., pp. 33-37.

5. See the editorial by Roger C. Palms, "Promiscuous," *Decision*, 22, No. 6, (June 1982), p. 13.

1
The Fear Barrier

Objection: "I'm Afraid."

Scripture Lesson: Jeremiah 4:22; 2 Timothy 1:3-14

Introduction

The devil is in the business of erecting barriers to prevent us from sharing our faith. He is the architect of a giant obstacle course to witnessing. One of the most formidable barriers which he throws before us is fear. The fear factor is usually caught up around the objection: "I'm afraid."

A poll taken at a Billy Graham Crusade in southeastern Michigan asked the question: "What is your greatest hindrance in witnessing?" Fifty-one percent answered that it was fear of how the other person would react.[1]

An article which I read some time ago suggested seven possible reasons pastors resist pastoral calling in the homes of church members. Two of the seven had to do with fear. The author suggested pastors may fear closeness or criticism. The desk and the pulpit enable us to maintain a certain distance. We do fear listening to criticism because it makes us vulnerable and carries pain with it.[2]

Apparently, some of us don't witness because we are afraid of being rejected, afraid of being hurt, afraid of being offensive, or afraid of failure. It is even possible that we are afraid of being bitten by a dog. Two of my former students, while witnessing from house to house, were both bitten by different dogs on the same day. It was a painful experience for them. That kind of experience can take the wind out of one's sails.

Most Do Not Reject Us

Let me share with you several things which I have found helpful in overcoming fear. First, the overwhelming majority of persons do not reject us when we encounter them with the gospel. On the contrary, they welcome our concern and treat us with respect and courtesy. Some even receive our message with much joy. Less than one percent of the persons I have encountered in my witnessing have been rude, foul-mouthed, insulting, threatening, or violent. So, the chances are about ninety-nine in a hundred that when we share in the right spirit, we will be received in the right spirit.

Those who do not welcome us, or who do not respond positively to our witness, are not necessarily rejecting us personally. They may only be rejecting our message, or our style. That, they are free to do. It is a part of human dignity that one is free to say no even to his or her Creator. To put it a bit more strongly, one is free to go to hell if he or she so chooses.

The Aroma of Christ

That brings me to a second thing which has helped me to overcome the barrier of fear. Witnessing is somewhat like spreading the fragrance of a great perfume. In fact, Paul said that God "through us spreads the fragrance of the knowledge of him everywhere. For we are the aroma of Christ to God among those who are being saved and among those who are perishing" (2 Cor. 2:14-15).

The problem is that not everyone likes the smell of our perfume. As Paul put it, we are "to one a fragrance from death to death, to the other a fragrance from life to life" (2 Cor. 2:16). No wonder the apostle went on to exclaim, "Who is sufficient for these things?" (2 Cor. 2:16).

When we offer ourselves as living sacrifices to God, the sweet savor of our sacrifice which rises up to God for all to smell will turn some on and some off. The smell of that Christian perfume will bring life to those who are being saved but death to those who are perishing. Hence, our very vocation of witnessing has a built-in factor which may arouse the hostility and opposition of the powers of death and darkness.

That there is an intrinsic negative aspect to the gospel which turns some persons off cannot be denied. The good news is foolishness to some and a stumbling block to others. I know that I am not sufficient to bear such a heavy fragrance. And yet I must, for love leaves me no other choice. This recognition of the negative power of my perfume helps me to break through the barrier of fear.

A Proper View of Success

A proper view of what success is has also helped me to break the fear barrier. There is really no such thing as failure in witnessing. The only possible failure involved in witnessing is the failure to witness, the failure to take advantage of the opportunities which God gives us to share.

Success in witnessing, therefore, is taking advantage of our opportunities. It is being faithful to Christ. It is being, doing, and telling whatever we can. If we go as far as we can, that is success by God's standards.

I do not say that success has nothing to do with numbers and statistics. However, the Christian witness will not define success by the worldly standards of victory, salesmanship, and fame.

Witnessing is not collecting scalps to brag about among other Christians. Nor is it adding new notches to our evangelism gun. Rather, witnessing is sharing with others what God has done for us through Christ. It is making disciples. Therefore, I do not fear failure nearly so much as I fear unfaithfulness to my opportunities and possible infidelity to the gospel. I do not wish to operate at the level of "peddlers of God's word" (2 Cor. 2:17).

Short-Term Versus Long-Term Gains

Still a fourth thing which helps me to break out of the fear barrier is the idea of investing for long-term gains as over against short-term gains. The witness who is overly concerned with short-term gains should be afraid of becoming offensive.

When we are too anxious for short-term gains in our witnessing, we run the risk of using disgraceful and underhanded ways. We open ourselves to the possibility of practicing cunning and manipulation and tampering with God's Word (see 2 Cor. 4:2). The pressure to succeed by the world's standards may move us toward an instantism in witnessing which results in the loss of integrity.

Persons who use offensive methods and styles in witnessing are usually playing the averages rather than investing for long-term gains. They are more concerned with getting their converts in the front door than they are with keeping them from exiting by that same door or by some other door.

If we invest for long-term gains in our witnessing, we shall not get uptight about immediate results. We shall relax and leave the results to God. "Obedience is our responsibility," writes Joyce Neville; "results are God's responsibility."[3]

A Continuum of Receptivity

Everyone can be located on a continuum of receptivity to the gospel. That is a fifth idea which keeps me from getting too uptight and fearful in my witnessing. If a scale of gospel receptivity is constructed, which moves progressively say from zero to ten, some of our potential disciples will be at ten and others at zero. Some will be at five and others at seven.

We can't expect the person on the lower end of that scale to be as responsive to our witness as the person who is on the higher side of the scale. Success, when measured by such a scale, might be moving a person from point zero to point one or from point seven to point eight.

Jesus himself said of one individual that he was not far from the Kingdom, but of another he labeled him a prodigal who lived in a far country. Modern principles of communications teach us that it is unreasonable to expect the same response from the "distant" person as from the "close" person. Therefore, when we are prone to say, "I'm afraid I'll be rejected" or "I'm afraid I'll fail," let us remember not every potential disciple is at the same place on the receptivity scale.

The Role of the Holy Spirit

A sixth thing which helps me break through the fear barrier is my understanding of the role of the Holy Spirit in witnessing. Paul told us that "God did not give us a spirit of timidity but a spirit of power and love and self-control" (2 Tim. 1:7). Paul even connected this kind of spirit, which I understand to be the Holy Spirit, with witnessing. "Do not be ashamed then of testifying to our Lord" (2 Tim. 1:8).

Only through the assistance of God's Spirit can we ever be equal to the task of being the aroma of Christ (see 2 Cor. 2:14-16). The

Holy Spirit is no spirit of fear or timidity. He is the Spirit of power. We need not fear the face of any person. We need not be intimidated by any individual. He who is in us is greater than he that is in the world.

Pastor Martin Niemoeller told how he became aware of being free of fear. He was called before Hitler in 1934. Niemoeller realized that Hitler was scared. Hitler said: "Every time I drive out of the gate of the Reich Chancellery, I have to be prepared in case somebody has a revolver and is planning to shoot me." The führer was actually more afraid than the pastor who stood before him. That's when Niemoeller recognized that he was not fearful.[4]

The image of the Christian witness as Mr. Milquetoast cowering and bowing down and backing up from others is patently false. On the contrary, the witness who is filled with the Holy Spirit is filled with the dynamite of God. He or she is a powerhouse for God. The Spirit-filled witness is outfitted with the whole armor of God (see Eph. 6:10-20) and is therefore prepared to stand victoriously and to speak boldly for Christ. I do not marvel then that the queen of England feared the prayers of John Knox more than she feared an army of soldiers!

The Servant-Master Relationship

Furthermore, we need to take very seriously the fact that the servant is never greater than his or her Master. "Truly, truly, I say to you, a servant is not greater than his master; nor is he who is sent greater than he who sent him," said Jesus (John 13:16). This is a seventh factor which may help us to break loose from the barrier of fear.

Many times in lay witness training events, I have inquired of participants their major reason for not witnessing. Often the answer has been, "I'm afraid I might get hurt." I want to answer, "Well, so what? Is the servant ever greater than his Master? Can the one sent ever be greater than the One who sends him?"

A certain fear of getting hurt physically can be healthy. That's one reason for doing witness visitation in teams of threes rather than alone or in twos. There is some physical safety in numbers. Nevertheless, an inordinate fear of being rejected or insulted is improper and out of place.

It may help us to recall that the word *witness* comes from a Greek root meaning martyr. There is an ultimate risk of martyrdom in Christian witnessing. There is a place for suffering in witnessing. Paul counseled us to "take our share of suffering for the gospel in the power of God" (2 Tim. 1:8). If we are indeed persecuted on account of Christ, rather than on account of our own insensitivity and ignorance, let us rejoice and be glad (see Matt. 5:10-12). We are no better than those witnesses who have gone before us and no better than our Lord who was reviled and crucified.

Well might that carving on the memorial honoring the Confederate dead in Edenton, North Carolina, be applied to all Christian witnesses who are faithful unto the point of death:

> Gashed with honorable scars,
> Low in glory's lap they lie,
> Though they fell, they fell like stars,
> Streaming splendour through the sky.

Jacob Burckhardt long ago said: "Christianity is suffering." Indeed it is!

Experience and Knowledge

One additional answer to overcoming fear should be mentioned. George E. Worrell suggests that ignorance and the lack of experience are roots of much fear about witnessing. "Nothing," says Worrell, "will help to take the fear out of witnessing more than doing it."[5]

I have found that to be true in my experience. The fear seems to vanish in direct proportion to our knowledge and experience. The more we witness, the more we realize that most of our fears are unfounded. The more knowledge we gain about witnessing, the more confident and bold we become.

A part of our problem with fear is that so many of us do not have even one self-conscious, intentional track on which our witnessing can operate. What Jeremiah said of Israel may be said of us, "They are skilled in doing evil, but how to do good they know not" (4:22).

I have discovered that a witnessing track built around the letters FORM has helped me and my students overcome some of our fear and anxiety about faith sharing. Those letters FORM of course yield the word *form*.

The *F* stands for *family,* the *O* for *occupation;* the *R* for *religion,* and the *M* for *message*—the message of the gospel. My objective is to share the message of the gospel with potential disciples. However, before the witness train can reach its destination, it usually has to engage in some friendly conversation about family and home. Also, it passes through (and occasionally stops) at stations *O* and *R.*

If you don't have a better track on which to operate, I recommend the FORM structure to you. Something just that simple may get you through the barrier of fear.

Conclusion

It is a matter of historical record that America's westward frontier was settled by rugged individuals who were able to overcome many barriers. They overcame the natural barriers of mountains, rivers, deserts, ferocious animals, and inclement weather. They triumphed over the human barriers of hostile Indians and renegade outlaws. They took the West because they were victorious over the barriers of their own spirits such as fear and loneliness.

The world is full of success stories about persons who never permitted the fear of failure to control their actions. If Colonel Sanders had been afraid of failure, he would not have started Kentucky Fried Chicken after his retirement. If Harriet Tubman had been afraid of failure, she would never have started the underground railroad. If the Wright brothers had been afraid of failure, they would have never invented the airplane. If Helen Keller had been afraid of failure, she would never have been released from her dark shell of deafness, dumbness, and blindness. If Marie Curie had been afraid of failure, she would never have discovered radium. If Jonas Salk had been afraid of failure, he never would have developed the Salk vaccine.

There is really no such thing as failure in evangelizing. Sincere workers never fail. A pastor baptized a woman in Calgary, Alberta. He asked her who led her to Christ. The lady said: "A woman of your church who called on me five years ago, and I declined her invitation. But after she left, I was so disturbed that I had to face the issue. Six months later I gave my heart to Christ in my own home. But because of our absence in the country, this has been my first opportunity to confess Christ."6

I think C. B. Hogue spoke the truth when he said, "The greatest enemy of witnessing is fear." The final answer to overcoming fear is love. "There is no fear in love, but perfect love casts out fear. For fear has to do with punishment, and he who fears is not perfected in love" (1 John 4:18).

One final small tip for dealing with fear is to make a resolution that just for today you will not be afraid. You may be able to deal with the problem of fear for one day at a time whereas you can't cope with it a whole week, month, year, or lifetime.

Notes

1. Leighton Ford, "What Are You Afraid of?" *Decision*, 19, No. 12 (Dec. 1978), p. 4.

2. See Neal A. Kuyper, "Are Pastors 'Called' to Home Visitation?" *Christianity Today*, Vol. XXIV, No. 20, 21 Nov. 1980, p. 38.

3. Joyce Neville, *How to Share Your Faith Without Being Offensive* (New York: Seabury Press, 1979), p. 31.

4. See the editorial interview " 'What Would Jesus Say?' " *Sojourners*, 10, No. 8, (Aug. 1981), pp. 13-14.

5. George E. Worrell, *How to Take the Worry Out of Witnessing* (Nashville: Broadman Press, 1976), preface.

6. This true story is related by Arthur C. Archibald, *New Testament Evangelism* (Philadelphia: Judson Press, 1946), p. 107.

2
The Perfection Barrier

Objection: "I'm not good enough."

Scripture Lesson: Genesis 17:1; Matthew 5:48

Introduction

A frequent excuse which I have heard for not witnessing is, "I'm not good enough." Other expressions of this major barrier to witnessing are: "I've got enough problems of my own which I need to work on"; "When I get myself straightened out I'll start witnessing"; and "I am just not up to it right now." Whatever verbal form this barrier takes, it seems to boil down to one of four things.

False Humility

Sometimes "I'm not good enough" indicates a false humility. Genuine humility is always desirable, but a bogus humility can become injurious to our spiritual, mental, and physical health. The apostle Paul advised us "to think with sober judgment" about ourselves (see Rom. 12:3). It is just as important for us to think highly enough of ourselves as it is that we not think too highly of ourselves. Thinking of ourselves too lowly is as dishonest as thinking too highly.

The "I'm just a nobody" mentality won't cut it in evangelism. Many persons hide behind this attitude without even knowing it. They may even be under the impression that this is genuine humility. You are somebody. To belittle ourselves when God has so richly endowed us may be a form of blasphemy. We need to affirm our importance and value before the face of God.

Moral and Spiritual Inferiority

Most of the time, however, the "I'm not good enough" objection means "I'm not good enough morally or spiritually." Immediately

we have to answer: "Of course you're not! No one is except God!"
Jesus told the rich young ruler who called him "Good Teacher"
that "No one is good but God alone" (Mark 10:18).

If we wait until we become good enough to start witnessing, we
shall never begin in this life. Moral and spiritual perfection await
another world called heaven. You will never get perfect until you
have been glorified.

The Christian life is an Abrahamic pilgrimage. We call three of
the way stations in that journey of faith justification, sanctification,
and glorification. If you are a Christian, you have been justified;
you are being sanctified; you will be glorified.

The New Testament witnesses didn't wait until they became
morally and spiritually perfect before they started bearing witness
to Jesus Christ. Paul called himself the chief of sinners, but in spite
of his sins he became an itinerant evangelist to much of the Roman
Empire. Would anyone claim that Simon Peter was perfect? Yet
he took the gospel to Cornelius and his household and to many
more besides. Both Peter and John were uneducated, common
men, but they said to the Council: "We cannot but speak of what
we have seen and heard" (Acts 4:20). They were under a divine
compulsion to bear witness to the Christ.

The New Testament churches and Christians did not wait until
they were perfect to witness. We are prone to idealize them. But
they were no more perfect than are we. Some of the same problems which face us confronted them. Thank God they did not wait
until all their problems were solved before moving out to the lost
world with the gospel of peace.

God did tell Abraham, even when he was one year short of being
a hundred years old, to "be blameless" (Gen. 17:1). One never gets
too old to be holy. Jesus did tell his disciples to "be perfect, as your
heavenly Father is perfect" (Matt. 5:48). But he didn't mean they
were to be complete and mature morally and spiritually before
they uttered a witnessing word or performed a witnessing deed.
"We must not wait until we are holy before we move to serve,"
said A. C. Archibald. "Rather we must begin with what we have."[1]

On the other hand, one of the best things you may have going
for you in evangelism is your sense of inadequateness. If you
thought too highly of yourself, that would be a dreadful and almost

insurmountable obstacle to your effectiveness. Overconfidence in the flesh will bring a great fall and defeat.

Some of us who strut like peacocks in the church need to repent. Instead of acting like trustees of the new Jerusalem, we ought to repent in sackcloth and ashes.

You are right to realize that your life and your lips, your walk and your talk, ought to agree. You are right in believing that your life ought to witness. Some Christians forget that their words can be empty unless the Word becomes flesh in them. Disciples are not born; they are born again. Disciples are made. They are followers of Jesus Christ. You do have to have a testimony in order to bear witness.

You are surely right in recognizing that your life is not good enough to do all of your witnessing. The person who says "I'll just let my life witness for me" is insufferably self-righteous. No one is that good. That to which we bear witness must always be greater than ourselves. We and others may always find some fault in ourselves, but we will find no fault in Jesus. He is the only one without sin.

Those who think they are not good enough to witness are correct in thinking that we need to practice what we advocate. One United States senator in 1981 visited the White House to plead for protection for the U.S. shoe industry. He forgot that he was wearing a pair of Italian-made Guccis. When the press accepted his invitation to inspect his wardrobe, they found shoes from England, Germany, and Italy as well as the good old USA. That same senator launched a crusade to limit Japanese auto imports in 1981 while two German Mercedes sat in the senatorial garage.[2]

Doubtlessly, many unbelievers can agree with what Shelley, the poet, said: "I could believe in Christ, if he did not drag behind him that leprous bride of his, the church." When Sam P. Jones had thoroughly understood the people on his first circuit, he became seized with this conviction: either there were two kinds of Christianity, or else the majority of his people had religion and he didn't; or, he had it and they didn't. He decided to confront his congregation with their inconsistencies and to express his honest thoughts toward them. One of his sayings was that he had rather

be Bob Ingersoll and disbelieve the Bible than to be a professing
Christian believing everything, and living just like Ingersoll.[3]

Now having said all of that, I must nevertheless agree with John
Chrysostom's observation that teachers who do not practice what
they teach should nevertheless keep speaking in the hope that one
day they will be converted by their own words.[4] Then, too, I ask
you to ponder these wise words about God from Frederick
Buechner: "When he does his work through human beings, they
are apt to have feet of clay . . . because that's the only kind of
human beings there are, saints included."[5]

Human Elements in Witnessing

A third form which this perfection barrier seems to take relates
to the human elements in witnessing. Some who say "I'm not good
enough" are putting themselves down with a false humility. Others who say "I'm not good enough" may be saying, "Unless people
see my angel wings I can't witness." But there may also be those
who say "I'm not good enough" and mean by that a reference to
human factors such as eloquence, patience, the ability to listen to
others, discipline, personality makeup, etc.

Bertha Conde wrote a book which I hope to read one day. Its
title is what intrigues me: *The Human Elements in the Making of
a Christian.* A. C. Archibald, who experienced so much success as
an equipper of lay evangelists, at times used Conde's book as a text
for his six-week training sessions.[6]

I shall not attempt to single out all of the human elements in
witnessing. Let it suffice to comment on several of these factors.

Eloquence and keen intellect are human factors in witnessing.
Archibald has some advice for those who are not witnessing because they aren't eloquent and may not be geniuses. "God does
not need eloquence—it may be an encumbrance; he does not
require keen intellect—it may only be a temptation to argumenta-
tion."[7]

Ability to listen to others is a human factor. Studies by Lyman
K. Steil of the University of Minnesota indicate that we typically
listen at only 25 percent of our capacity. The good news is that we
can sharpen our listening skills. One thing we can do is to take
notes while we are listening. We can take notes even while listen-

ing in a telephone conversation. Probably we ought never to answer a telephone without pen and paper in hand.

Another thing we can do is plan to report the essence of what we hear to someone. Further, we might take action to minimize or eliminate distracting forces. For example, we might turn down the television, or the radio, or close the door. Moreover, we should always be on the lookout for valuable material in what is being communicated. Finally, we should identify those words and ideas which are emotional triggers for us. When emotionality is high, listening is usually correspondingly low.[8]

Tenacity and daring are human factors. This anonymous poem speaks to those elements:

> God has his best things for the few
> Who dare to stand the test.
> God has his second choice for those
> Who will not have the best.[9]

The Physical Factor

There are also occasions when the perfection barrier focuses upon the physical factor of the imperfect human body. While this could be viewed as another of those human elements referred to above, it is important enough to single out as a fourth form which the perfection barrier may take.

When some prospective witnesses object, "I'm not good enough," they mean to say that they are not good enough or beautiful enough physically. Perhaps they have some deformity of body or a severe physical handicap. Somewhere they may have gotten the false notion that only those who are "number ten" in body can actively bear witness to their Lord. I think our culture tends to make us think that even God can't use a man unless he has an Arnold Schwartzeneggar body or a woman unless she has a Farrah Fawcett figure. How foolish, and yet how very real!

I would remind you that there is a word of Scripture about "eunuchs who have made themselves eunuchs for the sake of the kingdom of heaven" (Matt. 19:12). Eunuchs are certainly physically deformed. Luke's story of the conversion of the Ethiopian eunuch (see Acts 8:26-39) shows the gospel crossing a significant physical barrier. Eunuchs are not only welcome in the kingdom of God; they can be witnesses to God's reign.

Paul's "thorn in the flesh" may have been a physical problem such as poor eyesight or some other infirmity of body (see 2 Cor. 12:7-10). God did not remove Paul's thorn in the flesh, but that didn't prevent him from excelling as a missionary evangelist.

We don't let our physical limitations keep us from pursuing business success. Why should it prevent us from sharing our faith? Take Bobby Denning of Mount Olive, North Carolina, for example. Denning started a little business in a smokehouse with a dirt floor. That business has grown and expanded until today it is a million-dollar company. Denning was crippled by muscular dystrophy at age ten and had to quit school while in the third grade. That's when he began his business in the smokehouse on his family farm near Grantham. He started tinkering with neighbors' radios. His only "employee" way back then was in the first grade. Now that Denning is forty-three, that first-grader is still working with him.

Denning's motto is: "I'm known by the customers I keep." He works very hard to encourage repeat sales in his stores. In 1982 he was named North Carolina's Small Businessman of the Year. And little wonder because he says: "I don't feel that anyone is any more handicapped than they consider themselves to be."[10] That kind of attitude about our physical handicaps may enable us to turn what we had thought were witnessing liabilities into witnessing assets.

Additional Suggestions

One simple but important thing we can do to overcome the perfection barrier to witnessing is to use more testimonies from rank-and-file Christians in our churches. We have a lot of heroes that we never hear from. Public testimonies offer us an opportunity to listen to some of God's unsung heralds. Also, if we can get those stories in print and on radio and television, we can unveil more of them to the church and to the world.

Here is just one illustration. Ron Lamb of First Baptist Church, Tucker, Georgia, has an unusual witnessing ministry. He is a modern-day good samaritan who rescues auto drivers in distress. Because Tucker is a suburb of Atlanta, Lamb has ample opportunities to use his mechanical skills on the cars of stranded motorists.

Year-round, Lamb, dressed in coat and tie, maneuvers his hulking, rust-spotted tow truck through rush-hour traffic to and from his job as a US Post Office supervisor. He is a welcome sight to surprised motorists with an overheated radiator, a broken fan belt, or a flat tire.

When Lamb spots a stranded car, he stops and offers to help. If he can't fix the car, he tows it to someone who can. All of this is done free of charge.

Everybody at Lamb's church was talking about using their gifts for the Lord. "I knew I couldn't preach," said Lamb, "but I knew I could change a tire and drive a truck." He bought a road-worn tow truck, replaced the engine, added new tires, and overhauled the winch. Since then, day and night, he has aided dozens of marooned motorists.

Lamb donates gasoline, hoses, belts, clamps, antifreeze, oil, and even starters. If he gives gas to a motorist, he also gives the can provided the recipient will promise to refill it and give it to someone else who needs it. While doing all of this Lamb openly and boldly tells folk about Jesus Christ and explains his ministry. What a great combination of both deed and word in evangelism![11] That's the kind of model with which many Christians can identify.

Another suggestion for breaking down the perfection barrier is that we need to set a "par" for the witnessing "course." When par is reached, let it go at that. If par is perfection, we shall never reach it. You may say, "I'm not perfect, just forgiven." That reflects a healthy attitude and recognizes your own shortcomings.[12]

Conclusion

Each generation of Christians makes the preceeding generation complete. Hebrews 11:39 says, "apart from us they should not be made perfect." Completion rather than moral perfection is what the writer has in mind. No generation of Christians is complete in and of itself. Only we can make it complete as we become living links in that chain of witnesses reaching from them to us, and from us to the succeeding generation.

Our credibility as witnesses is not established by our mental, moral, spiritual, physical, or social perfection. Our effectiveness as witnesses to the gospel of the kingdom of God does not depend on our being good enough. Rather, both our credibility and our effectiveness are established by our obedience to him who said, "you shall be my witnesses" (Acts 1:8).

Notes

1. Arthur C. Archibald, *New Testament Evangelism* (Philadelphia: The Judson Press, 1946), p. 112.
2. See the editorial "Booted," *The Kansas City Times,* 19 June 1981, p. A-16.
3. Mrs. Sam P. Jones and Walt Holcomb, *The Life and Sayings of Sam P. Jones,* 2nd. rev. ed. (Atlanta: The Franklin-Turner Co., 1907), p. 67.
4. John S. Mogabgab, rev. of *Spirituality of the Beatitudes,* ed. Michael Crosby, *Sojourners,* 10, No. 6 (June 1981), 34.
5. Shirley and Rudy Nelson, "Buechner: Novelist to 'Cultural Despisers,' " *Christianity Today,* XXV, No. 10, 29 May 1981, p. 44.
6. See Archibald, *Evangelism,* p. 87.
7. Ibid., p. 84.
8. Beth Ann Krier, "When Listening, Few People Are All Ears," *The Kansas City Times,* 12 Feb. 1981, pp. A-1 and A-12.
9. Archibald, *Evangelism,* p. 134. No attribution or author is cited by Archibald.
10. Joan Oleck, "Businessman Builds from Dirt Floor to Honors, Million-Dollar Company," *The News and Observer,* 17 Mar. 1982, pp. 1A and 9A.
11. See "Ministry to 'Broke Down,' " *Home Missions Notebook,* 2, No. 4 (Winter 1981), p. 10.
12. Win Arn and Charles Arn, "Six Steps to Effective Disciple Making," *Church Growth: America,* 8, No. 1, Jan.-Feb. 1982, p. 5.

3
The Spiritual
Gift Barrier

Objection: "I don't have the gift."

Scripture Lesson: Zechariah 4:1-14; Ephesians 4:4-16

Introduction

Another objection to witnessing which I have heard increasingly during the last twenty years is, "I don't have the gift." The advent of this objection began with the renewed emphasis on the gifts of the Holy Spirit in the 1960s and 1970s. Most persons who raise this barrier are saying, "I don't have the gift of an evangelist." Some, however, are saying, "I don't have the gift of witnessing." Others mean that they don't have the gift of the Holy Spirit. A few even mean that they don't have the gift of evangelism. Let us confront these four aspects of the objection in reverse order.

The Gift of Evangelism

Only by inferences can the Bible be said to teach that evangelism is a gift. There are three major lists of spiritual gifts in the New Testament (Rom. 12:6-8; 1 Cor. 12:8-10, 27-31; Eph. 4:11). Only one of these lists mentions "evangelists" as a gift. That is in Ephesians 4:11, and even then the word *evangelism* is not used.

Therefore, "evangelists," and not evangelism, are said to be one of the gifts which the risen Christ bestows on his church. Evangelism is not a spiritual gift so much as it is a function, mission, or activity of the church. It is no more a spiritual gift than is education, worship, missions, stewardship, or ethics.

Even in the Ephesians reference some take "evangelists" as more strictly an office than as a gift. I do not personally see that much distinction between an office and a gift. And perhaps we should be quite charitable toward those who fail to see much difference between a function and a gift. Nevertheless, if we iden-

tify evangelism with disciple making, then it is more a command
than a gift (see Matt. 28:19). Also, if we see evangelism as advertis-
ing the wonderful deeds of God in Christ, then it is more a mission
than a gift (see 1 Pet. 2:9*b*). Moreover, if we view evangelism as
the ministry of reconciliation, then it is more a ministering function than a gift (see 2 Cor. 5:18).

Evangelism is unmistakably a charismatic function of the
churches. But we may not be on firm ground in calling it a gift.
If when you say, "I don't have the gift" you mean that you don't
have the gift of evangelism, one possible answer is: "Of course you
don't. Nobody really has the gift of evangelism as such. That is one
of several necessary functions of the church."

Insofar as evangelism is a legitimate function of the church, it
is incumbent upon us all. Evangelism is not a gift which God
bestows merely upon the "spiritual" members of a congregation.
Even if it is not your "thing," you can't escape responsibility for
a wholesome and intelligent evangelism in your church.

The Gift of the Holy Spirit

Now if when you say, "I don't have the gift," you mean that you
do not have the gift of the Holy Spirit, we need to examine that
very closely. Paul said that no one can say "Jesus is Lord" apart
from the Holy Spirit (see 1 Cor. 12:3). If you are a true disciple of
the Lord Jesus the Holy Spirit has blown upon you, brooded over
you, breathed upon you, brought you into newness of life, birthed
you into the family of God, and baptized you with fire from heav-
en.

We do indeed encounter persons in our churches today who are
like those twelve disciples of John the Baptist at Ephesus. They
said to Paul, "No, we have never even heard that there is a Holy
Spirit" (Acts 19:2). There are those who have been baptized into
somebody else's name, or for someone else's sake, rather than into
the name of the Lord Jesus. I am persuaded that many of those
who have received what they call the baptism of the Holy Spirit
in our time are like those disciples of John. Some of them have
never been saved. What they are experiencing in some cases
sounds and looks like the new birth.

Some who have been strangers to the gift of the Holy Spirit explain their newfound power and joy in terms of now accepting Christ as Lord, whereas in the past they had only accepted him as Savior. Theologically it is impossible to separate Jesus' saviorhood from his lordship. But popular theology and its expression frequently varies from biblical and systematic theology.

The apostle Peter said in his sermon on the day of Pentecost: "Repent, and be baptized every one of you in the name of Jesus Christ for the forgiveness of your sins; and you shall receive the gift of the Holy Spirit" (Acts 2:38). That promise of the outpoured Spirit is to us and to our children. It is even to those who are far off from God and to everyone whom the Lord our God calls to himself (see Acts 2:39). Joel the prophet said God would pour out his Spirit upon all flesh in the last days. He was even more specific, including our sons and daughters and both our male and female servants (see Joel 2:28-29).

If you have not received the gift of the Holy Spirit, perhaps you have not been born of the Spirit. If you aren't a Christian, repent of your sins and believe in the Lord Jesus Christ. A part of your birthright as a Christian is the gift of the Holy Spirit. Noncharismatic Christians—Christians without the Holy Spirit—are contradictions. Claim your birthright as a citizen of God's kingdom. Recall that precious word of Paul: "When we cry, 'Abba! Father!' it is the Spirit himself bearing witness with our spirit that we are children of God" (Rom. 8:15-16).

If you know you are a disciple of Jesus Christ, but you are not filled with the Holy Spirit, forsake all known sin and ask God to fill you with power from on high. Seek his face in prayer. Ask and you will receive. Seek and you will find. Knock and the door of his storehouse will be opened to you. We are filled with the Holy Spirit in the same way we are saved, namely "by hearing with faith." We began with the Spirit; let us not think that we shall continue or end in the flesh (see Gal. 3:1-5).

The Christian life is life in the Spirit. We can't be very effective witnesses to Jesus Christ until we receive the gift of the Holy Spirit, or unless we are empowered by the Spirit.

The Gift of Witnessing

Now, let us consider this barrier from another vantage point. When you say, or hear someone else say, "I don't have the gift" and mean you don't have the gift of witnessing, I need to tell you that witnessing is nowhere in the Bible called a gift. You are on very thin ice walking around on such an excuse. Every Christian fills the role of a witness to Jesus Christ. Christian witnessing is really every Christian's "thing." If you have been crucified with Christ on the cross, buried into the watery grave with him, and raised to newness of life, you have a story to tell. You are a firsthand witness to his mighty deeds in your life.

Sure, you may not be an ordained pastor or evangelist. But you were ordained as a witness and a priest in your baptism. A. C. Archibald, as a very young minister just out of college and seminary, became pastor of a large church in the southwestern United States. Two weeks after his arrival, 1,000 census cards were placed into his hands. On those cards were the names of citizens in that community who were not members of Archibald's church but who expressed a preference for it. The church had already held its annual revival meeting. What was the new pastor to do with those cards?

Archibald called a meeting of his deacons and official board to see if they could decide what to do with the prospects. No one seemed to know what to do. They floundered around until the guest of one of the deacons, who was himself not a member of that church, arose and suggested that the men organize themselves into teams of twos and go out after those thousand persons and win them to Christ. The guest told how over the past five years he had been used of God to lead sixty-five men to Christ and into the churches. He in fact passed around a book with the names of those sixty-five men for the deacons and church officials to see.

Pastor Archibald seized the man's suggestion as a word from the Lord. They all went to God in a spirit of prayer. Fifty teams began to search for those 1,000 persons. Night after night they went out in the homes and day after day into the offices. On the sixth Sunday, those teams had brought to Christ and led into the church

132 out of the 1,000. And still others were added as the weeks and months passed.

When Archibald left that pastorate, a timid little man who had scarcely opened his mouth since the day he had become a Christian in a tent meeting said: "I will always thank God for your pastorate with us. I have been a Christian for twenty years and, so far as I know, I never asked a man or woman to become a Christian. And now, in one year, my friend and I have been used of God to win five men to Christ and the church."

That was the beginning of A. C. Archibald's long and fruitful emphasis on the use of lay Christians to win others to Christ. "The laymen are our last reserve to save the world," said Archibald. "The hour of the layman has struck."

Archibald even supposed that "Jesus and all his apostles were laymen." By 1946, this great equipper of lay evangelists had seen at least 2,000 lay evangelists in action. And those 2,000 had before his eyes won and brought to Christ and the church over 4,500 persons.[1] What a story! And it's all true, not fiction but fact. If A. C. Archibald could do that in his day, how much more than that can you and I do in our day?

You don't have to have formal ordination as an evangelist or pastor or missionary in order to be a fruitful witness to Jesus Christ. We are told that H. A. Ironside was never formally ordained. But he pastored Moody Memorial Church in Chicago for over eighteen years. Some have called Ironside the "Archbishop of Fundamentalism." This tireless witness in his prime averaged forty weeks a year on the road itinerating for Christ.[2]

A person can do *almost* anything he or she wants to do. I shall even dare to say categorically that one *can* do anything God calls him or her to do. Why, I even read an inspiring story of a lady with no arms who became a dentist. She was in her second year of dental school when her arms were burned off in an encounter with high-tension electrical wires. Now she teaches preventive dentistry and oral disease control.[3]

If we want to be effective witnesses, love will find a way. I have read of one church in Oregon that can trace eight "spiritual generations" of persons who have been discipled and in turn discipled another.[4]

The Gift of An Evangelist

That brings me again to those who say, "I don't have the gift."
There are indeed those who mean by that objection that they do
not have the spiritual gift of an evangelist. And let me say to you,
if that is your point, "You may be right. Perhaps you don't have
the spiritual gift of an evangelist." Peter Wagner says, "The average Christian church can realistically expect that approximately
10 percent of its active adult members will have been given the
gift of evangelist."[5]

Three times this word *evangelist* is used in the New Testament.
Paul told Timothy, "do the work of an evangelist" (2 Tim. 4:5).
Philip, one of the seven, is called "the evangelist" (Acts 21:8).
Ephesians 4:11 uses the term in the plural as one of Christ's gifts
to his church for body building. As used in those contexts, an
evangelist in the apostolic age seems to have been a kind of pio-
neer missionary who broke up new ground for Christ and planted
churches in virgin territory. I find it suggestive that the only person actually called an evangelist in the New Testament was Philip,
apparently a layperson even in our sense of that word.

I have heard of a man who led at least one person to Christ every
day for seven years! My guess is that such a man would have the
spiritual gift of an evangelist. I see this vital spiritual gift as belong-
ing to those Christians who can effectively confront others with
the claims of God upon their lives; who do it with joy, finesse, skill,
and respect for personality. All evangelists can do this one on one,
and some can do it with large gatherings of persons. It does seem
to me that those who are mass evangelists like Billy Graham also
have some other spiritual gifts such as prophecy or teaching.

Granted that you may not have the gift of an evangelist, that
doesn't mean that there is nothing you can do to lead the lost to
Christ and into his church. Far from it. Eddie Cantor once entertained a group of orphaned children. While candy and toys were
being distributed, he noticed a little girl in the rear of the room.
She was very sad. Her expression contrasted with the joy of the
other children. He went over and said, "Honey, you don't seem
to be having a good time here. Is there anything I can do for you?"

She replied, "Love me." You and I can always love persons even if we don't have the gift of an evangelist.

And in addition to that, we can make ourselves available to others. Availability is a trait which we need in our evangelizing. It is called *disponibilité* in French and *disponibilita* in Italian, meaning the holding of oneself or anything in readiness until the time for which it is called. Bank deposits, for example, are to be held available or on call.

Three things are involved in availability. First, there is a receptivity to God and to others which means I am truly present to him and to them. Second, an ingredient of gentleness is displayed toward persons and events. Third is an inward attentiveness.

Receptivity which is truly present involves all of our faculties: body, mind, and soul. It includes an active listening. We have to endeavor to get inside the other thou in this I-thou relationship. Malcolm Muggeridge, the noted British writer and commentator, said the thing which is so startling about Mother Teresa's work with the wretched persons of Calcutta is that she is totally present to every human being. Her total presence is evidenced whether in relating to a baby discarded in a garbage can, a leper, an aged sick person who is dying, or any kind of derelict. You and I need to be available to God and to others like that.

Gentleness is not on the world's agenda. One leading department store, for example, carried a full-page newspaper ad in the mid-1970s about a book, supposedly a best-seller, which taught persons how to be successful through intimidation. All you have to do to win, according to the ad, is to intimidate your opponent. The assumption is that persons are basically adversaries. How radically different was what Isaiah and Jesus said: "he will not break a bruised reed/or quench a smoldering wick" (Matt. 12:20; also see Isa. 42:3). Again, Jesus said, "Blessed are the meek, for they shall inherit the earth" (Matt. 5:5).

Evangelism needs that gentleness which is exhibited in handling a newborn babe, a sick child, a fevered head, a lover's hand, and a person involved in an accident. When we experience the vulnerability of others, we should respect that vulnerability with a reciprocal gentleness. Someone has translated that Beatitude which reads "Blessed are the meek" as "Blessed are those who don't go around kicking in people's doors!" Such gentleness enables us to hear God's footsteps, and not to violate our neighbor's personality.

Beyond gentleness and a receptivity which is genuinely open to God and others, our availability involves an inward attentiveness. This is a sensitivity to the faintest whisper of God. It is a willingness to live life by the nudgings of the Holy Spirit. Only a finely tuned instrument will be tuned to the frequency of God's Spirit.

When we are available with this kind of inward attentiveness, we may be drawn to persons even across great distances. Some person or burden may be on our heart. A sudden impulse to speak to a person may come over us. There may come some flash of insight into another person or into their problems. We shall be free to engage in the ministry of affirming others.

Part of the power of the early Christians seems to have come through their availability at the right time, to the right persons, in the right places. Three illustrations of this availability may be seen in the ministry of Philip (Acts 8:26-40), that of Ananias (Acts 9:10-19), and of Peter (Acts 10:1-33,44-48).[6]

Conclusion

I suspect that many who say, "I don't have the gift," have experienced what we call burnout. That is not only a problem with vocational workers in the churches. It's a big problem with lay workers too.

Some of that burnout is due to having left our first love. Do you know what an "Ephesian" is? That is one who has left his or her first love. The one who held the seven stars said to Ephesus, "you have abandoned the love you had at first" (Rev. 2:4).

Notes

1. Arthur C. Archibald, *New Testament Evangelism* (Philadelphia: The Judson Press, 1946), pp. 24-27. See all of chapter 2, "I Entered the New Way," pp. 23-27.
2. See " 'Harry' A. Ironside," *The Sword of the Lord,* XLVIII, No. 7, 12 Feb. 1982, p. 10.

3. See "The Accident that Challenged My Faith" by Margaret Jones Chanin as told to John Warren Steen, *Decision,* 22, Nos. 8 & 9 (Aug.-Sept. 1981), p. 7.

4. Gary L. McIntosh, "A Biblical Standard of Success," *Church Growth: America,* 7, No. 4 (July-Aug. 1981), p. 13.

5. C. Peter Wagner, *Your Spiritual Gifts Can Help Your Church Grow* (Glendale CA: Regal Books, 1979), p. 177.

6. William P. Clemmons, *Discovering the Depths* (Nashville: Broadman Press, 1976), pp. 30-36. I am indebted to Clemmons for almost all of this material on availability.

4
The Professional Barrier

Objection: "That's a minister's work."

Scripture Lesson: Proverbs 11:30; Ephesians 4:7-16

Introduction

A Sunday School teacher learned how to share the gospel through the use of a marked New Testament. He had a class of teenage boys. His plan was to visit every lost member of his class and to share the gospel with them. He got so excited about the response of several boys to his presentation that it showed all over his face.

It was on his next visit that the wind was knocked out of his sails. The thirteen-year-old boy was not the problem. He was ready and eager to become a Christian. It was the boy's father who was offended. The father told the teacher, "That's a minister's work." He upbraided him for his audacity and made it clear that he didn't think anyone except an ordained minister with appropriate training should ever attempt to do personal evangelism.

I was that Sunday School teacher's pastor. It shocked and saddened me. That was my first and abrupt introduction to one of the most formidable barriers to witnessing I have encountered. I have heard the same objection voiced in similar ways: "I don't believe a layperson can do that"; "Witnessing is too important a matter to trust to a layperson"; "We pay our pastor and church staff to do our witnessing for us," and "You have to be in church to do that."

Some Unordained Witnesses

You don't have to be an ordained minister and have a degree in theology in order to lead persons to Christ. D. L. Moody was never ordained, but he led thousands to Christ. According to John R. Mott, the great turning point in Moody's ministry came when he heard Henry Varley say: "The world has yet to see what God will do with a man who is wholly consecrated to him." Moody then and there determined to be that man.

He was ungrammatical in his speech and letters, but he didn't let that keep him from being sold out to God. His voice was rather flat, but his faith in God was fat. Moody made it a rule of his life never to let a day pass without speaking to someone about his or her soul's salvation. Do we dare make such a rule for ourselves?

Charles Haddon Spurgeon was one of the greatest pastor-evangelists of the nineteenth century. Yet Spurgeon was never ordained. His lack of a formal ordination didn't keep him from winning many hundreds of persons to faith in Christ.

You may be thinking, "Well, I'm no Moody or Spurgeon." You don't have to be. As a matter of fact it was a salesman by the name of Edward Kimball who introduced Moody to Christ; A. C. Archibald told how a woman of cultural limitations won twenty-two young women to Christ in one year. Also, he related how an insurance agent won twelve men to Christ in a single year.[1] These two persons were not spectacular or super Christians. They were folk like most of you. If they could do it, you can do it too.

A Christian layman, who belonged to a small Baptist church in Kansas, dropped into a noonday meeting in Kansas City. He heard a man say, "No Christian ought to be comfortable so long as a single unsaved person remains in his community." He pondered that statement. It made him uncomfortable. The matter was taken to God in prayer. That layman was so shaken that he could never be the same again. There was born in his soul a deep conviction that he ought to speak to others about Christ.

He was a traveling man, so he had many opportunities to share with others. Little by little he was able to lead men to make a definite decision for Christ. He was really surprised at the positive response which he got. His power of presentation grew. Within two years that ordinary layman had the extraordinary joy of seeing 122 men confess their faith in Christ. While he did business for himself, he was also self-consciously on business for the King.[2] If that man could do it, you can do it too.

Samuel H. Moffett and his wife were visiting in a Korean village. Mrs. Moffett asked a merchant how much a watermelon cost. The merchant was so surprised at finding a foreigner who spoke Korean that at first he was struck dumb. He even forgot to tell her the price. There was something more important he wanted to say. He asked, "Are you a Christian?" And when she replied, "Yes," he smiled all over. "Oh, I'm so glad," he said, "because if you weren't, I was going to tell you how much you are missing."[3] If that Korean merchant could do it, you can do it too.

What You Have

What do you have by way of equipment which you may use as a lay evangelist?

- You have your Christian education since childhood or conversion.
- You have your Christian character which you are seeking to perfect into the likeness of Christ himself.
- You have your knowledge and understanding of the way of salvation.
- You have your personal experience of the preciousness of Christ as your Savior and friend. That is your testimony and your spiritual autobiography.
- You have a knowledge of the plan of salvation such as may be seen in John 3:16 or in a few verses from Romans 3; 6; and 10.
- You have the gift of the Holy Spirit who goes before you and with you.
- You have the prayers of God's people for the lost. These include your own prayers, those of your prayer partners, the pastor, and unknown prayer warriors whom God has raised up throughout his church.
- You have your deep sense of concern for the lost. One writer called that concern, "the most potent instrument on earth in winning a soul to your Saviour."
- You have above all your own God-given personality. In other words, you have *you*, your mind, attitudes, experience, and your ways of speaking and thinking.[4]

It is so easy for us to overlook the small things in our witnessing. We tend to focus on what we don't have more than on what we have. Some of the characters in Matthew 25:31-46 overlooked the importance of giving water to the thirsty, food to the hungry, clothes to the naked, and visits to the sick and imprisoned. George Buttrick used to say, "There is no lost good." Others may forget but God never does. "When saw we . . . ?" If you didn't see it, God did.

You may be thinking of some grandiose things you have to do in order to bear witness to Jesus Christ. Don't do it! Think of the little things you can do. Don't overlook something as simple as speaking a word of encouragement to a friend or giving an appropriate book to someone you know.

One of my former students went back home from college for a weekend visit. He was not a Christian then. But his best friend had become a Christian and sought to lead him to Christ. He refused Christ at that time thinking his dear friend would also soon turn away from Christ and the church. He watched his friend closely. Instead of turning away from Christ and the church, the friend surprised him by becoming more deeply committed.

That friend gave him a little book which contained several of Billy Graham's sermons. As he read those sermons, the Holy Spirit convicted him of his sin and his need for the Savior. He said, "I felt as though Billy knew me personally and was preaching just to me." The sermons told him how to become a disciple of Jesus Christ. Before he had finished reading the book, he had opened his heart to Jesus and invited him to come in.[5]

You don't have to be a big professional to win persons to Christ. You have to be your best self and use the resources God has given you in the natural, normal course of your daily life.

The Parable of the Clown

Sören Kierkegaard, somewhere in his writings, told about a traveling circus that moved from town to town in his native Denmark. One afternoon they had set up on the outskirts of a village and about forty-five minutes before the performance was to start, the tent caught on fire. It so happened that the clown was the only one in the troup fully dressed. So he was dispatched into the village to get help.

He did his job extraordinarily well. He appraised everyone he encountered of the emergency and implored their assistance. However, the problem was that he was dressed as a clown, and across the years people had developed certain expectations of clowns. They concluded that all these wild antics and talk of fire were simply a new way of drumming up a crowd. It was not until they looked on the horizon and saw the ominous red glow that they realized that he was not doing a clown act at all, but he was a human being bearing an urgent message.[6]

Reflect for a moment on that parable of the clown. Who does the clown represent? I can tell you this: you don't need a clown's suit and paint to make you an effective witness for Christ. One of the greatest things you have going for you is your "lay" status. They expect the church staff to go out and share their faith. Some think that's what they're paid to do. But when a nonprofessional who earns his livelihood at some secular occupation intentionally shares his or her faith, you will be more effective than Kierkegaard's poor clown.

Archibald believed that people were not reached because lay-persons had not planned to reach them. Mr. J. was an actual case in point. Archibald called six of his men together in a council to decide what to do about Mr. J. Mr. J. was a prominent insurance man. He was a regular attendant at the church. His wife and a daughter were members of the church. He attended and that was all. The council discussed every angle: background, attitudes, present interest, disposition, and temperament. Finally, after prayer they decided that Mr. G. and Mr. F. were the men best fitted to approach him. They consented to go. The date was set. They would report back three nights hence.

The team went to see Mr. J. the next day by appointment in his office. After a few pleasantries, they came right to the point and invited Mr. J. to accept Christ as his Savior and to join the church. Mr. J. was silent for a while. Then, that successful insurance man expressed surprise that two laymen would come to see him on such a mission. He invited them to come to his home the next night and to bring the pastor with them.

They all gladly made the visit in Mr. J's home at the appointed hour. There in the presence of his wife and daughter Mr. J. readily confessed his faith in Christ. Not only did Mr. J. join the church, but five years from that date he was serving as Sunday School director for his church.[7] One wonders how many persons there are attending our churches like Mr. J. who would readily accept Christ if faithful laypersons would seek them out privately and extend the invitation.

Every Christian a Minister

Those who raise the professional barrier do not know that every Christian is a minister. They have a "high church" mind-set which contradicts the New Testament doctrine of the priesthood of all believers.

Findley Edge, an outstanding leader of the lay movement among Southern Baptists, has identified two major insights which became the focus of his life. Very simply, these insights were that God's basic call is a call to ministry, and that the ministry of the laity is basic to this calling. These two insights became the foundation of Edge's understanding of the gospel and of his philosophy of religious education.[8]

Several weekly church papers which I have seen list alongside the heading of "Minister" the words "Every Member." Then alongside the heading of "Pastor" the pastor's name is given. That is an effort to bear witness to the belief that every Christian is a minister. The word simply means a servant, not a professional vocational minister who is highly trained. Our evangelism ought to be lay-centered and pastor-supported rather than pastor-centered and lay-supported. There is no way under heaven that we can pay our pastors or our church staff to do our witnessing for us.

The best time for us to teach and implement the truth that every Christian is a minister is probably when one is converted to Christ and joins the church. Mary Cosby of the Church of the Savior in Washington, D.C., tells about one of their new converts. He was a gentleman well over seventy when after years of resistance he finally surrendered to Christ and joined the church. Later, this gentleman told Mary he had been disappointed only once after he had joined the Church of the Savior.

"Like what?" asked Mary.

"Oh, I don't know," he said, "but I was a *new person*, and I thought that the day I joined, maybe you would come up and say,

'Well, Bill, we need a man in Algeria; pack up now, you leave in the morning.' "

"Bill, would you have done that?" asked Mary.

"Of course I would have done it. I was a new creation!"

Instead of being asked to go to Algeria, Bill was asked to serve on the usher committee. Mary Cosby correctly observes that there is nothing wrong with asking one to serve on an usher committee, unless your man is ready to go to Algeria![9]

The Equipping Ministry

One of the most helpful things which can be done to break down the professional barrier to witnessing would be for the professional ministers to take their equipping ministry more seriously.

"One wonders," wrote Archibald, "how far the failure of the clergy to enlist the layman in active Christian work is responsible for our present evangelistic decline."[10] Some pastors seem to prefer to do all of the personal evangelism in their congregation. They refuse to show their members how to be effective witnesses.

Here is what I mean by the equipping ministry. Elton Trueblood, the Quaker philosopher, was asked in 1981 how he recalled the origins of the lay movement. He answered "A great turning point occurred on January 1, 1950." On that date, Stephen Neill, a missionary and an Anglican bishop of India, spoke to an inter-seminary conference at Rock Island, Illinois, on "The Equipping Ministry." Neill got the phrase from the fourth chapter of Ephesians. "So far as I know," said Trueblood, "that phrase had not been used up until that time."[11]

That's what I mean by the equipping ministry, what is said in Ephesians 4:11-12,

> "And his gifts were that some should be apostles, some prophets, some evangelists, some pastors and teachers, to equip the saints for the work of ministry, for building up the body of Christ."

I see the full-time and part-time paid church staff ministers as functioning primarily to equip the rest of God's people for their work of ministry. All of us are called to ministry, but some of us are called and gifted in the equipping ministry.

Notes

1. See Arthur C. Archibald, *New Testament Evangelism* (Philadelphia: The Judson Press, 1946), pp. 83-84.

2. Ibid, pp. 58-59.

3. Related in *Evangelism News*, Summer, 1979, p. 6, a quarterly newsletter of the Office of Evangelism and Renewal, Episcopal Church Center, 815 Second Avenue, New York, N. Y. 10017.

4. These are adapted and revised from Archibald, *Evangelism*, p. 113.

5. This was related by Ralph Dale in an unpublished research paper which he did for me in M4500, Basic Evangelism, at Southeastern Baptist Theological Seminary, fall of 1981. See especially pp. 4-5.

6. Related by John R. Claypool, "Seeing or Stereotyping," *The Baptist Program*, Feb., 1981, p. 13.

7. Condensed and adapted from a true story related by Arthur C. Archibald, *Evangelism*, pp. 135-136.

8. See the interview with Findley Edge by Bill Bangham, "The State of the Laity," *World Mission Journal*, 52, No. 12 (Dec. 1981), p. 4.

9. Mary Cosby, "Now!" *Seeds*, 3, No. 11 (Dec. 1980), p. 6.

10. Archibald, *Evangelism*, p. 16.

11. See the interview with Elton Trueblood by Charles Lawson, "The State of the Laity," *World Mission Journal*, p. 11.

5

The Model Barrier

Objection: "I'm no Billy Graham."

Scripture Lesson: Psalm 107:1-3; 1 Peter 2:18-25

Introduction

Many times I have heard Christians say when asked to share their faith, "I'm no Billy Graham." That's the model barrier which must be overcome if more of the rank-and-file citizens of the kingdom of God are to become intentional witnesses for Jesus Christ.

A Preliminary Answer

A preliminary answer to this objection is: "Of course you're not. You're not expected to be. God wants you to be yourself."

Let me set you free. You don't have to be a minature Billy Graham, an echo of Billy Sunday, or be overwhelmed by the stature of D. L. Moody to be an effective witness for your Lord.

God only needs one Billy Graham. And besides, he is not in the cloning business. Evangelist Billy Graham was himself asked in 1981: "Which is more important, mass evangelism or one-on-one evangelism?" He answered: "One-on-one evangelism. In my judgment, there is no such thing as mass evangelism—that's a misnomer."[1]

It's okay for you to want to put your best foot forward in witnessing. That's altogether appropriate in evangelism as in etiquette. But God does not expect you to be someone you're not or to become someone you can't be. Your best self will be very pleasing to him. He'll even take you just as you are, warts and all.

Most Evangelists Are LayPersons

Actually, most evangelists are lay folk just like you. I find it instructive and inspiring that L. R. Scarborough, in his *With Christ After the Lost,* acknowledged a debt of gratitude "to Doc Peques, now with the Savior, whose tireless zeal in going after the lost as an untrained layman, fanned into flames the holy fires of evangelism in his own soul."[2] Scarborough was saying that an untrained layperson had stirred up the fires of evangelism in his own soul.

Have you ever looked at Acts 1:8 in the light of Acts 8:1? Consider for a few moments those two verses:

- Acts 1:8—"But you shall receive power when the Holy Spirit has come upon you; and you shall be my witnesses in Jerusalem and in all Judea and Samaria and to the end of the earth."
- Acts 8:1—"And Saul was consenting to his death. And on that day a great persecution arose against the church in Jerusalem; and they were all scattered throughout the region of Judea and Samaria, except the apostles."

Acts 8:1 is in some ways a fulfillment of the promise in Acts 1:8. That is especially true of the scattering throughout Judea and Samaria. However, it was not the apostles who took the gospel to Judea and Samaria. They stayed in Jerusalem. Rather, it was the rank-and-file members of the church who "went about preaching the word" (Acts 8:4).

Stephen, one of the seven, became the first Christian martyr. He was himself a lay witness who became one of the goads against which Saul of Tarsus kicked. Indeed, the apostle Paul may be said to be an answer to Stephen's prayer. Following this deacon's death, it was those who were scattered abroad who spread the gospel to Judea and Samaria. Philip, another of the seven, is an example of evangelizing by early lay Christians (see Acts 8:4-40).

I find it educational and suggestive that Philip, a layman, is the only person whom the New Testament calls "the evangelist" (see Acts 21:8). We have no New Testament warrant for believing or teaching that all evangelists are in a special category labeled "clergy."

God uses ordinary persons to be his witnesses. You don't have

to be extraordinary in the sense of being supertalented, superedu-
cated, superoutgoing, supersharp, etc. Please believe that little is
much when you yield it to God and use it for his glory.

Do you remember January 13, 1982, when Air Florida's Flight
90 crashed on takeoff from Washington's National Airport and fell
into the icy waters of the Potomac River? Martin Leonard Skutnik
III, age twenty-eight, by sheer chance happened to be on the
scene. He stood with other spectators on the riverbank. A woman
survivor was struggling in the cold water. Skutnik plunged into the
river and rescued her.

He had never taken a life-saving course, but he saved the lady's
life. Nor did Lenny Skutnik stop with that. Although half-frozen
himself and the possible victim of frostbite, he gave his dry coat
to another survivor who was suffering from two broken legs.

Skutnik was identified as a former meat-packer, house painter,
furniture plant worker, hamburger cook, and strip-and-wax man.
At that time he was a general office worker in the congressional
budget office. He had a wife and two children and lived in a rented
town house. In other words, he was what you might call Mr. Average American. But he couldn't stand by idly and let another help-
less human being die without trying to help. He became our hero
on that fateful day by risking his life and health to rescue another
human being.[3]

I believe some of our most effective rescuers of the perishing
and the dying are Christians about as unknown and as unsung as
was Lenny Skutnik before January 13, 1982. Some of God's unsung
heroes may well be those faithful lay fishers of persons whose
names and deeds are unknown to us and to our historians.

You Are Royalty

You may not be a Billy Graham, but if you are a Christian you
are royalty. The secular assault on Christian values may be seen
most in the devaluating of persons.

Our children and young people are told almost from the time
they are born that certain brand names in clothing are better than
others. Look what has happened with designer jeans. We convey
the message to persons that if you're going to be accepted, you've

got to wear someone else's name. Little wonder that persons are confused about their identity.

What we need to do is tell persons that the only brand name they need to wear is "Christian." The name that really matters in our modeling is that of Jesus Christ.

We are royalty you know. The sons and daughters of King Jesus are princes and princesses. He has made us so. His word to us on this is that we are a "kingdom" of "priests" (see Rev. 1:6). We are not merely priests; we are "a royal priesthood" (see 1 Pet. 2:9). That word *priest* in Latin is *pontifex* meaning literally a bridge builder. Therefore, you and I as Kingdom citizens are God's royal bridge builders. We are those in the service of King Jesus who build the bridges across which others come to God.

I can say of that what the old country boy said: "If that doesn't ring your bell, then your clapper must be broken." Not all of us have the opportunity or natural ability of an Einstein, a Salk, or a Schweitzer. But within each of us there is a spark that can light a creative fire, if we will use it.

You Can Do Something

You may not be a Billy Graham, but there is something you can do for your Lord. The psalmist said, "Let the redeemed of the Lord say so" (Ps. 107:2). If God has gathered you to himself and rescued you from the land of darkness, you can say so with your lips.

We sometimes so emphasize dynamic evangelists like Billy Graham that even some of our preachers have said to me in so many words, "I'm no Billy Graham," I agree with evangelist Sam P. Jones that earnestness is more important in a preacher or a speaker than powerful logic and finished rhetoric. Jones said:

> Earnestness cannot be feigned. It is just like the natural and health-ful glow on a maiden's cheek compared to the artificial coloring. Earnestness can always be distinguished from emotional gush or bellowing hurrahism. Earnestness is a thing of the eye and face more than of the voice or the words.[4]

If we are in dead earnest about sharing our faith, God will deliver us from "witnessing lockjaw," and loosen our tongues to tell of his reality, greatness, and goodness. Telling others what God has done for us is one thing that most of us can do even if we aren't accomplished public speakers.

Do you know what FMD is? Foot-and-mouth disease has long been one of the world's most serious animal diseases. Veterinarians call it FMD for short. Finally, a genetic breakthrough has been developed by scientists which promises to cure FMD through a vaccine.[5] No such vaccine has been developed which we can give to Christians suffering from another kind of FMD. But love and a strong desire to be used of God will go a long way toward moving our feet and loosing our tongues with the gospel of peace.

Some of us can go to the lost and lead them to the Savior. They will not come *here.* We have to go *there.* They will not come to us. We have to go to them.

"They're waiting for us out there." That statement was made by a lay witness who drove eighty miles to witness to a sick man. This witness had promised the sick man's son that he would go and see his father. The son couldn't go because he was in prison. The witness went and the sick man was saved.

We can all intentionally serve God through our daily work. An inscription on a tombstone in a small village cemetery in England reads: "Here lies the body of Thomas Cobb, who made shoes to the glory of God in this village for fifty years."[6] In these days of shoddy workmanship and declining production, the Christian can set an example for quality and industriousness in his or her labor. As citizens of God's government, we are to live and work by the Golden Rule, "whatever you wish that men would do to you, do so to them; for this is the law and the prophets" (Matt. 7:12).

Some of us can self-consciously bear witness to others through our pens and our typewriters. Frederick Buechner (pronounced Beekner), for example, has been writing for thirty years. He has published seventeen books, only one of which was a best-seller—*A Long Day's Dying.* Writing is more than a craft for Buechner; it's his ministry. "I think I'd write," says Buechner, "even if there were nobody to read."

Buechner addresses two different kinds of audiences. His nonfiction works are aimed at persons like a congregation in church; whereas his fiction seeks to reach persons who wouldn't be caught

dead in a church. He aims his novels at the people whom Schleier-
macher called religion's "cultured despisers."[7]

Some of us may also work through our local churches with orga-
nizations such as Prison Fellowship. Prison Fellowship, a ministry
to prisoners founded by Charles Colson in 1976 following the
Watergate scandal, has grown now to more than 100 full-time
staffers in thirty-five states. The fellowship's budget is nearly $3
million.

One unique feature of Prison Fellowship is its network of Community Care Committees. These are volunteers from the outside
who spend a day each week teaching Bible classes, offering emotional support, and writing letters for inmates. Many of these
volunteers come from conservative evangelical churches.[8]

Others of us can simply become friends to the lonely and the
lost. Remember Mrs. Browning's request to Charles Kingsley:
"Tell me the secret of your life, so that I may make my life beautiful too." Kingsley's reply was, "I had a friend."

You may indeed not be a Billy Graham, like that great mass
evangelist through whom God has blessed so many, but there is
something you can do to spread the faith however small and insig-
nificant it may seem to you. On Sam P. Jones's first circuit, one of
the wealthiest members was taken ill and thought he was going to
die. He sent for the pastor to come and pray with him. Jones went,
and when he entered the sickroom the member said, "I have sent
for you to pray for me."

"Well," said Jones, "I don't see any good reason for asking the
Lord to heal you. If you can tell me any reason why you should
live, I'll pray for you; so far as I know you have never done anything for the Lord that I can stand upon, while praying. You have
paid absolutely nothing to the assessments of the church; none of
the missionary money for home or foreign cause has been paid by
you; the stewards can't get anything out of you towards my salary;
wife, children, and myself have needed the necessaries of life, and
my horse has had nothing much to eat, and you have an abundance of everything here in your home, and feed in your barn, and
could have helped us; therefore, I don't see anything to stand
upon. There is no use in my asking God to restore you; I can ask
him to forgive and save you, and take you to heaven; but, there

is no reason why I should ask him to preserve your life; as you are absolutely worthless to the cause."

The member answered: "You are right. There is no reason why I should live, but I will make you a promise if you can stand upon that."

"Very well," replied Jones, "what is the promise?"

He said, "I will see that my assessment is paid in full, and that you have the things that you need for your table and horse."

Jones did then pray for the man's healing. He fully recovered before long and kept his promise, much to the surprise of his neighbors. This gentleman paid his vow and became one of the warm friends and supporters of Jones during his stay on that circuit.[9]

Called to Model

Whatever we may do to bear our witness to the Savior, we are called to model after him who is the perfect model evangelist, Jesus Christ. He is our example that we should follow in his steps, said Peter (see 1 Pet. 2:21). Although we are no Billy Graham, we are called to be extensions of the incarnation of Jesus Christ. We are to be, as Martin Luther said, a little Christ to our neighbors.

A model is really an analogy. The analogous mode of learning may well be the most productive. Analogies give us possibilities for comparison and contrast. Take holiness for example. That is an abstract idea. However, when you can say, "That person is holy," then you have an analogy. Because that person is holy, if indeed he or she is, you can compare yourself to that person.

One thing which Christians can't delegate to others is their modeling role in evangelization. One minister of youth, who has coordinated nineteen youth mission teams to eight countries, contends: "If students are to catch a vision for the world, the church must first provide models who have such a vision."[10]

Ananias and Sapphira probably gave more than any one of us. They died because they were phonies. They did not model after Jesus Christ.

Conclusion

Have you ever failed? If you are alive, you have. I heard a preacher tell how he held forth for thirty minutes on blind Barabbas. So long as our standard and model is Jesus the Christ, we shall never attain perfection in this life. But only as we pattern after his perfect example, and after those who imitate him, do we have a chance of overcoming the model barrier to witnessing.

Notes

1. See the interview "Candid Conversation with the Evangelist," *Christianity Today*, XXV, No. 13, 17 July 1981, p. 20.

2. L. R. Scarborough, *With Christ After the Lost* (New York: George H. Doran Co., 1919), pp. vii and viii.

3. James J. Kilpatrick, "Rescuer's Name Could Be Legion, for He Is Many," *The Kansas City Times*, 22 Jan. 1982, p. A-9.

4. Mrs. Sam P. Jones and Walt Holcomb, *The Life and Sayings of Sam P. Jones*, 2nd rev. ed. (Atlanta: The Franklin-Turner Co., 1907), pp. 64-65.

5. See the AP report, "Vaccine Developed for Foot-and-Mouth Disease," *The Kansas City Times*, 19 June 1981, p. D-8.

6. Robert J. Hastings, "Preaching on the Doctrine of Christian Stewardship," *Proclaim*, 1, No. 1 (Fall 1970), p. 23.

7. Shirley and Rudy Nelson, "Buechner: Novelist to 'Cultured Despisers,'" *Christianity Today*, XXV, No. 10, 29 May 1981, p. 44.

8. See "Colson Goes Back to Jail," *Newsweek*, 7 Sept. 1981, p. 41.

9. See Jones and Holcomb, *Sam P. Jones*, pp. 69-70.

10. Paul Borthwick, "Motivating Youth for Missions," *Christianity Today*, XXVI, No. 2, 22 Jan. 1982, p. 44.

6
The Time Barrier

Objection: "I just don't have the time."

Scripture Lesson: Psalm 118:24; Ephesians 5:16

Introduction

Almost every faithful witness to Jesus Christ has at some time had to overcome the time barrier in witnessing. How many times have you said, "I just don't have the time"? Most likely if you didn't say it, you heard someone else use that as a reason for not participating in intentional and structured faith sharing.

Busyness

Admittedly a lot of us are very busy these days. We are busy making a living, busy trying to make life worth living for ourselves and our neighbors, busy with recreation, education, civic clubs, children, church work, and a thousand other activities. Some of us are like Chaucer's sergeant of law. Nowhere are there others busier than we, and yet we seem busier than we really are. I agree with William H. Willimon that "How we spend our time tells something about our priorities and our personal needs and insecurities."[1]

How do most of us spend our time? Ted Turner, founder of the Cable News Network, said in 1981: "We spend 52 hours sleeping, 45 hours working, 14 eating, seven with personal hygiene and five in traveling to and from work" in a typical week. "And, according to Nielsen," continued Turner, "the average American spends 35 hours watching TV. That leaves only 10 hours for everything else."[2]

It is true that many persons don't have much spare time. I met a man in Detroit in 1981 who was working two regular full-time jobs. He was trying to make enough money to take care of his growing family. Those who work like that certainly don't have much time left for anything else.

Pastors are also caught up in the terrible busyness of our society. Many of them are overworked and underpaid. They too feel that they just don't have the time to do much self-conscious witnessing in order to make disciples.

It was that kind of response from pastors which prompted pastor A. C. Archibald to say: "The man who is too busy to win souls is too busy to be a minister. The minister must know more about evangelism, and actually *do* more about evangelism, than any layman in his church."[3]

Anyone who studies the life and ministry of Phillips Brooks knows how busy he must have been. He was beseiged by unconverted men and students who beat a path to his door. His friends urged him not to sacrifice so much of his time to them. However, Brooks said, "The man who wishes to see me is the man I wish to see."[4]

I tend to agree with William Feather who said, "We all find time to do what we really want to do." We do by and large control our use of time. We have not been placed into some mysterious time machine and made prisoners of time. Instead of time controlling us, we should seek to control it and make it our servant to enable us to do the will of God.

Another side of the busyness of our culture is the increasing leisure time and the new work arrangements which do give persons more quality time off from work. Trinity Lutheran Hospital in Kansas City for example has a new work plan for nurses called "7-70." Nurses work ten hours a day seven days a week, or a total of seventy hours a week. They get twenty-seven weeks off annually including a guarantee of three consecutive weeks off. There is no shift rotation and no rotation to other hospital units.[5]

Furthermore, no matter how busy we are, each of us has the same number of hours in the day. From the strict view of actual chronological time, you have as much time as does anyone else.

Seriousness and Urgency of Time

The Bible does give us some guidelines for the use of time. God takes time seriously, and so should we. He is the Creator and Lord of time. It was he who separated the light from the darkness, and who called the light day and the darkness night (see Gen. 1:3-5). He made the first day and all the days since. Augustine said that time was probably created at the same point in the divine career when the visible universe came into being.[6]

One aspect of time which we frequently overlook in our witnessing is the suddenness of our Lord's second coming. He will come as a thief in the night. His coming will be at an hour we do not expect. Therefore, we should be ready and seek to get everybody ready for his appearing (see Matt. 24:41-44).

The witnessing task is urgent because the final night is coming. One day, we know not when, the final curtain will fall on history. We should work diligently the works of the Son who has sent us because when that night comes "no one can work" (see John 9:4).

An anecdote of unknown origin tells about a man and woman from the North Carolina mountains who loved listening to a chiming grandfather clock. Once the clock went haywire and struck eighteen times instead of twelve at midnight. The mountaineer said to his wife: "Wake up, honey. We've got to do something quick. It's later than I've ever known it to be." There is a sense in which the Christian witness should always have that mountaineer's attitude toward time. Should we not forever cry out: "Awake, O sleeper, and arise from the dead, and Christ shall give you light" (Eph. 5:14)?

William Saroyan, five days before his death at age seventy-two, phoned the Associated Press saying, "Everybody has got to die, but I have always believed an exception would be made in my case. Now what?"[7] We need to remind ourselves and the rest of humanity that two things are sure, our own death and the coming judgment of God (see Heb. 9:27).

Yesterday is gone, and tomorrow may never be ours. Today is all we have. The psalmist said, "This is the day which the Lord has made; let us rejoice and be glad in it" (Ps. 118:24). That statement helps us to understand the everlastingness of today.

The preacher in Ecclesiastes assures us that there is "a time for every matter under heaven" (Eccl. 3:1). Surely if there is a time for every matter, there must be a time for faith sharing. That ancient witness assures us that there is "a time to keep silence, and a time to speak" (Eccl. 3:7).

Time as a Gift of God

Time is one of God's most precious gifts to us. We are stewards of time. That may account for the words of the psalmist, "So teach us to number our days/that we may get a heart of wisdom" (Ps. 90:12).

Maxine Hancock is certainly no lady of leisure. She is a homemaker, writer, and teacher who lives in Canada. Hancock has written: "The central attitude that controls my approach to time and its use is that *time is a gift* to be used to the glory of God."[8]

Each of us is living on borrowed time! All the days that we have, be they many or few, are borrowed from God. "This is the day which the Lord has made." I didn't make it. You didn't make it. God made this day. He made all the yesterdays. If tomorrow comes, he will make that day also. Every day is a day borrowed from God. God is the Lord of time and history. Our business is to rejoice and be glad in each borrowed day.

Hebrews 2:1 has an exhortation against failure to live up to our opportunity in God's redemptive purpose. The phrase is "lest we drift away from it." That is an unfortunate translation. The word really means to flow by. Hence, here it means "lest we be flowed by." We are the stationary ones. As the river of redemptive opportunities flows on, we are flowed by unless we seize these God-given opportunities and plunge into the flowing stream.[9]

Three Insights from Experience

My own time management leaves a lot to be desired. But let me briefly share three items which have helped me to better utilize my time. The first one is so simple that anyone can do it beginning right now. Stop watching TV. If you view it at all, let it be special programs of high quality and perhaps once or twice a week the news programs. Most of the programs aren't worth watching anyhow. They may also be dangerous to our spiritual health.

Second, I try to live by a personal spiritual discipline which I review every New Year's eve. My present discipline has twelve points to it; it is typed double-spaced on one regular size page. This discipline is a covenant which I renew annually with God. It gives structure to my daily life. I evaluate myself by it from time to time throughout the year. Something that simple may be what you need.

A third item which I have found helpful for several years now is to write out my personal work goals. Each New Year's eve I rewrite them or revise them in accordance with the light God has given me during the previous year. They serve as a kind of polar star around which I build my personal spiritual discipline. Again, they are typed on less that one regular page, although these are single-spaced. I have found them especially useful in prioritizing my use of time. They spell out what I believe to be God's dream for my life.

You can ask any well-disciplined person, "How on earth do you get everything done?" The answer will almost always be, "I don't." Nobody can do everything. What we have to do is arrange our lives into some kind of priorities. We Christians have to seek first God's kingdom (see Matt. 6:33). His rule and his righteousness should take precedence in our lives.

There is an old Chinese proverb which says: "There is nothing worthwhile accomplished without much pain." I have found that to be true in structuring my time to fit kingdom priorities.

Catching Time Robbers

"Take care of the minutes," said G. K. Chesterton, "and the hours will take care of themselves." Much as it is the little foxes who eat the grapes and are thus so pestiferous, so it is the little robbers of minutes which eat away our hours and our days.

If time management is a problem for us, we might analyze how we spend our time. We can do that by keeping a time log for at least a couple of weeks. Each day can be broken down into fifteen minute segments. We then record how each segment of the day is spent.

The next step in the process is to analyze our use of time using that time log. Particularly should we look for time robbers in the use of our days. Such time robbers as interruptions, unnecessary meetings, and lack of personal discipline should be singled out.

Finally, we might decide to work specifically to overcome one or two of those time robbers for a definite period of time.[10]

Definiteness is a missing element in so much of our evangelism. We do not have a definite prospect list. Nor do we have a definite time for visitation evangelism or definite teams of witnesses who have covenanted together with God, the church, and one another to go out and seek to win the lost. Also, we are often lacking in definite goals with definite time lines.

An Agenda Prescription

Andrew Carnegie, great steel executive and father of our public libraries, once asked a New York efficiency engineer what he could do to sleep soundly at night and also accomplish more at the office during the day. The simple, surefire prescription was to make an agenda of tomorrow's most important tasks, chores, errands, letters, and phone calls. Place the most critical at the top of the list. Then, don't fret anymore about tomorrow's problems. Instead, remind yourself that all your major tasks are already written down, which means you can quickly survey them in the morning without floundering around or wondering what to do next.

Carnegie asked the efficiency expert what the charge would be for his advice and was told to send him a check for whatever he thought it was worth. Soon Carnegie sent that engineer a check for $25,000 saying this agenda idea was the best thing he had ever tried to get more work done each day, and yet not be troubled by insomnia as he worried about what to do the next morning!

That may be your cup of tea. If so, drink all of it, and place on your agenda something about intentional faith sharing.

Additional Suggestions

Let me mention two other suggestions which may need to be expanded and fleshed out. Robert Schuller, one of America's well-known preachers, has a slogan which says, "Inch by inch, anything's a cinch." A lot of people laugh when they hear that. Nevertheless, it does make good sense. I think it may be based on the Chinese proverb which reads, "A journey of a thousand miles begins with one step."

Apply Schuller's slogan to the use of your time. Ideally and in reality, all of our time belongs to God. Still we have to decide exactly how to use it. If we only devote a few minutes of it each day to intentional witnessing, it will be a cinch to overcome the time barrier.

Paul in one of his sermons referred to David, who "after he had served the counsel of God in his own generation, fell asleep" (Acts 13:36). It is important that we servants of God seek diligently to serve our own generation. The evangelization of our generation is our responsibility. It is even possible when we overcome the time barrier for many of God's servants to serve future generations.

Conclusion

Some of us may never overcome the time barrier until we covenant with God and one or more other Christians to do highly structured evangelistic visitation and personal witnessing. But let us not forget that developing a witnessing life-style is our ultimate answer to conquering the time barrier.

Would anyone who knew Charles H. Spurgeon say he was not a busy man? That very name conjures up in our minds the power of a great pulpiteer. But we would do well to remember that a large part of Spurgeon's success was due to his personal work with individuals. For forty years in London, he averaged one convert a day, persons won outside his pulpit.[11]

We have to guard against letting the good become the enemy of the best in our use of time. Jesus was busy, but never too busy to bear witness to God's kingdom. He is our model in the use of time. When we Christians get too busy to witness self-consciously, we're too busy to please God.

Notes

1. William H. Willimon, " 'Time Robbers' and How to Stop Them," *Ministry*, 53, No. 9, (Sept. 1980), p. 9.

2. Steve Nicely, "Turner Uses NBC Show to Attack Networks," *The Kansas City Times*, 18 June 1981, p. C-2.

3. Arthur C. Archibald, *New Testament Evangelism* (Philadelphia: Judson Press, 1946), p. 29. Italics are Archibald's.

4. Ibid., p. 33.

5. See "10-Hour Days Have Benefits," *The Kansas City Star,* 20 Feb. 1981, p. 4C.

6. Harold B. Kuhn, "Cultural and Biblical Demands on Our Time," *Christianity Today*, XXV, No. 11, 12 June 1981, p. 59.

7. Quoted in the editorial "Saroyan," *The Kansas City Star,* 20 May 1981, p. 18A.

8. Maxine Hancock, "First Things First," *Decision*, 21, No. 9, (Sept. 1980), p. 8. Italics are the author's.

9. See Herschel H. Hobbs, *New Testament Evangelism* (Nashville: Convention Press, 1960), pp. 56-57.

10. See Willimon, *Ministry*, pp. 8-9.

11. Cited by Archibald, *Evangelism*, p. 33.

7

The Knowledge Barrier

Objection: "I don't know how."

Scripture Lesson: Jeremiah 9:23-24; Galatians 6:14-15

Introduction

The knowledge barrier is another formidable obstacle which has to be overcome for witnessing to be effective. This barrier centers around the objection: "I don't know how." At times the objection is voiced in this manner: "I don't know what to say or how to say it." A variation is: "I don't know how to talk to people." It often entails not knowing what outline or Scripture to use, and a lack of knowledge in how to meet persons and guide the conversation to the "big" talk about the gospel. This is a real obstacle in the minds and hearts of many would-be witnesses.

Some Don't Know How

My inclination is to take this objection at face value. Many don't know how. "The average church would like to do the work of evangelism, but it does not know how," wrote A. C. Archibald. "The average preacher is keenly desirous of exercising himself unto evangelism, but he is baffled at the 'how.' "[1]

If many pastors don't know how to win the lost, surely we should not be surprised that many rank-and-file Christians don't know how. D. James Kennedy, the founder of Evangelism Explosion, has told how he exhorted his people to share their faith when he began his pastoral work at Coral Ridge Presbyterian Church in Fort Lauderdale, Florida. It was not until Kennedy learned how to do personal evangelism and decided to show his people how to do it through on-the-job training that he became effective as an equipper of evangelists. It takes far more than exhortation to equip ourselves and others to share our faith.

However, we cannot automatically assume that those who voice this honest objection are thereby motivated to want to learn how. But enough of them do that we should make every possible effort to show them how. This objection points up the need for witness training for pastors and people.

The Knowledge of God

The essential knowledge in faith sharing is a personal knowledge of God. It is one thing to know *about* God but a quite different thing to *know* God.

Bishop Mortimer Arias of Bolivia said of his country, "Look, more than half of the population believe they are already Christian. They don't think that they need to know the gospel any more or any better. There is no more difficult people to evangelize than those."[2]

Part of our problem in evangelizing is that some of those who don't know how have no firsthand, intimate knowledge of God in Christ. The prophet Jeremiah said we should not glory in wisdom, or might, or riches, but in our understanding and knowledge of God (see Jer. 9:23-24). Paul would glory in nothing but the cross of Christ. To the great apostle, the new creation and crucifixion to the world counted more than circumcision or uncircumcision or any other thing (see Gal. 6:14-15).

H. Thomas Walker suggests five essential elements in an effective program of visitation evangelism:

- The visitor must have a faith to proclaim and know how to articulate it.
- He has to believe in and express confidence in the church as the body of Christ.
- He must have and express concern for the person he is visiting.
- He should be able to reveal and share his own experience of faith.
- He should be able and willing to help the prospect make a response to the challenge of the gospel.[3]

Notice that four of those five essentials relate to one's personal experience and knowledge of God. It is difficult to proclaim a faith we don't have. If you and I don't personally believe in the church as the body of Christ, how shall we get others to express their faith? If we don't have an experience of faith, how shall we reveal what we don't possess? If we haven't responded to the challenge of the gospel, what chance do we have of helping others to respond?

Prerequisite to knowing how to share our faith is our knowing God. An experiential knowledge of God through Christ is essential to effective witnessing. All other knowledge is built upon that foundational knowledge. God has in Christ unveiled to us the hidden treasures of darkness (see Isa. 45:3). In Christ are "all the treasures of wisdom and knowledge" (see Col. 2:3). That is the reason all evangelizing begins with the doctrine of the new birth, the new mind, the new heart, and the new creation. This "mystery" is not the secret knowledge of the Gnostic heretics. Rather, it is God's open secret made known to all in the good news of the kingdom of God.

Therefore, the first question which we need to ask ourselves and all who would be witnesses to the Christ is: Do you know God through Christ? Is your knowledge of God secondhand or firsthand? The great apostle Paul said to the Corinthians, "I decided to know nothing among you except Jesus Christ and him crucified" (1 Cor. 2:2).

Anybody who knows Jesus can bear witness to him. The woman of Samaria left her water pots and told her fellow villagers about Jesus. She had no training whatsoever. What she had was an illumination and a meeting with the Savior of the world.

Accurate Knowledge Is Important

We need to be very sure about the accuracy of that to which we bear witness. Even firsthand eyewitnesses can be wrong. This was powerfully illustrated by what happened to a South Carolina man during the Christmas season of 1980.

The South Carolinian was arrested in the middle of the night on Christmas Eve and charged with the murder of a police officer in New Jersey on that very day! Three eyewitnesses to the slaying in New Jersey picked the Carolinian as the murderer from a group of mug shots. One of the witnesses was a Catholic nun; another was a doctor; and the third a motorist. All three of them had been kidnapped and later released by the killer. They swear to this day that this was the man who kidnapped them and killed the officer! But, alas! Seventeen eyewitnesses swore that the accused murderer was at work with them in South Carolina during the very time of the slaying! Moreover, the company time clock record showed that the accused murderer was at work that day. Obviously this was a case of mistaken identity. Needless to say, the murder charges were dropped.[4]

Fortunately for us as Christian witnesses, we are not dependent upon the eyes alone for our facts and experiences. Our eyes see, our ears hear, our hands touch, our noses smell, and our tongues taste as it were him who is the Word of life (see 1 John 1:1-3). There are not just three or seventeen of us but a great company whom no one can count. Our character and reputation are beyond reproach. And we have not just experienced Christ once for a few minutes or a few hours, but our witness stretches from the year 4 BC to the present time, and it covers the whole earth rather than just one or two places.

Concern More Important Than Know-How

Having said all of that, I still contend that genuine concern is more important than exact know-how in witnessing. A. C. Archibald believed that "the most potent instrument on earth in winning a soul" to the Savior is a *deep sense of concern*. "If one has not that," said he, "no eloquence, position or brilliance will make him a soul winner."[5]

Archibald told how he had reasoned by the hour with a man in Lowell, Massachusetts, and had gotten nowhere. Along came a very humble but very godly man who approached the same lost person. After being browbeaten by the lost man's superior arguments and facile speech, the poor confused fellow broke down and with tears rolling down his cheeks said: "Mr. _____, I can't meet you in argument, I know. But I know my Saviour, and O sir, I have a terrible anxiety that makes me lie awake at night, I so want to see you a saved man." The prospect melted at once and gave his life to Jesus.[6]

There is no substitute for such concern. Much else may be missing; but if that passion is absent in our evangelism, we shall not lead many to our Lord. What we are really talking about here is that passion for the lost which reveals itself as *agapē* love in action by meeting the heartfelt needs of lost persons.

Evangelism without compassion is evangelism without power. We may need to pray, "God, break my heart with the things that break your heart."

Volunteers are usually more effective in God's army than are draftees. We seek workers with a willing heart. Conscription is out of harmony with the flavor of intentional evangelism.[7]

Some years back a man went beserk in New Jersey. He started shooting every man in sight. Many were killed and wounded. One man in a nearby office which was under attack grabbed a telephone and pulled it beside him as he dropped to the floor. He dialed the operator and begged, "For God's sake get the police up here. There's a man killing everyone he can. Please, hurry." The operator said, "I'm sorry you will have to call 411 to get that number."

During World War I a soldier was mortally wounded in no-man's-land between the two lines of trenches. He called for his friend to come and help him. The friend turned to his officer and said, "Sir, give me permission to go bring him back."

The officer said, "No! He will be dead by the time you get there." But the friend persisted. Finally the officer relented and said, "All right, go ahead." The soldier climbed out of the trench. He was hit by enemy fire. After a period of time he came crawling back toward the trench dragging the body of his buddy. The officer said, "What did I tell you? He is dead! And you are wounded! What did you accomplish?"

The soldier replied, "Sir, he was not dead when I got there. When he saw me, he said, 'You know, I knew you would come.'"

Many of our lost loved ones and friends and neighbors are counting on us. If our concern is deep enough, we shall not let them down. Our compassion will be revealed in our deeds. One of the easiest things in the world to do is to talk. But one of the most difficult things in the world is to communicate. *Agapē* love communicates in actions which back up our words.

Love and Do as You Like

Augustine reportedly once said, "Love God, and do as you like." The law of love is very powerful. If we genuinely love lost persons, we can use almost any legitimate technique and be effective in leading them to Christ.

The case of Mr. R. is unusual, yet not so rare that it doesn't in fact confront us from time to time. Mr. R. was president of the church choir, leader in the social and financial work of the church, as popular and unselfish and kindly a man as could be found in the congregation. The problem was that he was not a confessed Christian or a member of the church. Yet he was leading the music department—a whole department of the church work. And he was satisfied. The church had accepted him as he was. Why should he worry?

His name came before Pastor Arthur C. Archibald's council of six concerned advisors. Some of them even thought he was a member since he had for so long acted like one. They canvassed Mr. R. from every angle. Who was the most appropriate person to confront Mr. R.? They all agreed that this was a case for the pastor to handle.

Pastor Archibald invited Mr. R. to his office. He felt that his approach must be bold and sharp, but that he must speak the truth in love. Suddenly he turned to Mr. R. and said: "Do you know . . . that you occupy a very anomalous position in this church? You are assuming all the functions of a professed Christian and a church member, yet you are neither. You are playing a part."

The man's face flushed red. Immediately the pastor saw that he had hurt him. He picked up his hat and coat, came around to the pastor's desk and said, "I never expected to hear my preacher call me that. What was that word you used?"

"It was 'anomalous' " said the pastor.

"I have not said what I did to hurt you," the pastor continued. "I have had to call you up sharply that you may see where you stand. My deepest desire is that you may go all the way, having begun so well. I want you, having the forms of the Christian life and the standing in this church and community of a Christian man, to put reality into it by really being a Christian, by giving your heart to Christ, and confessing him before the world."

One week later, Mr. R. invited the pastor to come to his home. He met him at the door saying, "Pastor, when can I be baptized?" Immediately Mr. R. won his son to Christ. Both he and his son were baptized together.[8] Persons like Mr. R. can be won if they are approached by the right person in the right way and in a spirit of love. If one knows that we love him or her, we can say whatever is necessary and at least gain a hearing.

Learn by Doing

Up to here, I have made the points that some don't know how to share their faith and need to be shown how through show-and-tell witness training; the essential knowledge in faith sharing is a saving knowledge of God in Christ; accurate knowledge is important in witnessing; but genuine concern is more important than exact know-how. If we really love lost persons, they will tolerate most any legitimate technique. Now, let me go on to observe that one of the best ways to overcome the knowledge barrier is to learn by doing.

All the talk about what method to use may be a waste of time. The main thing is to go to it. It's like R. G. Lee said when someone asked him how to ride a mule. "The main thing is just go to it," said Lee.

I would do nothing to put down the spiritual disciplines of participation in public worship, Bible study, and prayer. But we may be deluding ourselves by thinking that Christian growth is achieved primarily through those disciplines. My feeling now is that Christian growth comes primarily through action and only secondarily through nurture. We grow most when we are intentionally bearing witness to Jesus Christ and deliberately involved in Christian service to others. A part of our problem may be that Christian nurture has become an end in itself, rather than a means to witness and ministry.

Cameron Townsend began his career in missions in 1917 when he went to Guatemala as a Bible salesman. He discovered that 60 percent of Guatemala's Indian population could not speak Spanish. So Townsend, with no linguistic training and no college degree, began to translate the New Testament into Cakchiquel.

It took him only eleven years. Today the same task usually requires two well-trained linguists an average of fifteen years. One linguist likened Townsend's effort to learning brain surgery with no formal training.[9]

If we want something badly enough, we shall be willing to pay the price. There are no shortcuts to success in the kingdom of God. A lady said after hearing two great pianists, "I wish I could play like that." Her husband retorted, "No, you don't." She said, "Yes I do." But her husband who knew her well said, "If you really wanted to play like that, you would be willing to pay the price."

The price of learning how to witness is to start witnessing self-consciously every opportunity God sends our way. If we want to know how badly enough, we shall learn by doing. We only appropriate our faith when we share it. Otherwise, we don't know our true identity or our real mission. Because God has planted in our hearts the seed of regeneration, we can't help but share our faith.

Only by fulfilling her mission to the world could Israel appropriate her election. Election is not a call to superiority but a call to service and mission. God's election is being repudiated when Israel refuses her mission. Gracious election is for service. The mission of the church is to proclaim God's mighty acts in Christ to the world. We learn how to fulfill our mission by being on mission all the time.

Some of you may be thinking, "Well, that could be very costly." Yes, we shall make mistakes when we learn by doing. The consequences could be serious. Nevertheless, Goerge Bernard Shaw's advice is still sound: "Nothing is worth doing unless the consequences could be serious."

Use What Knowledge You Have

A good beginning place in witnessing is to share as best we know how what knowledge we do have. One lady said, "Witnessing is to the Christian what fizz is to the Pepsi Cola."

There is an African proverb which says: "There is only one crime worse than murder on the desert, and that is to know where the water is and not tell." One reason God gave us the gift of speech is so that we could tell others about the wonderful love of God. If you don't know how to say something, you might remember that the shortest distance between two points is still a straight line.

A woman criticized Dwight L. Moody's preaching because of his faulty grammar. He replied: "You seem to have grammar good enough. What are you doing with it for the Lord?"

Pastor Roy O. McClain told about a man in China who came to a mission hospital and had cataracts removed from his eyes. All of a sudden the man left without telling anyone where he was going. He was gone for several weeks. Then one day that man came back to the hospital leading one hundred persons with a one-hundred-foot rope. They were all blind. He figured that if they could help him receive his sight, the others might also receive theirs at the same place.

Surely, each of us can tell others where we received our spiritual sight. At least we should be able to say, "One thing I know, that though I was blind, now I see" (John 9:25).

Leo Frank, a twenty-nine-year-old Jewish factory superintendent was convicted in Atlanta of killing Mary Phagan, age 14, one of his employees. That was in 1913. Frank was subsequently lynched by a mob. In 1982 Alonzo Mann, an eyewitness to the slaying, testified that Frank did not commit the murder. Instead, said he, it was the factory janitor who was the chief witness against Frank. The janitor had threatened to kill Mann who was at that time the fourteen-year-old office boy for Frank. Now, nearly seventy years afterwards, Mann said: "Many times I wanted to get it out of my heart. I feel a certain amount of freedom now. I just hope it does some good."[10]

What a haunting thing it must have been for Mann to keep that crucial knowledge to himself all those years. If he had shared his knowledge at the appropriate time, Leo Frank's life may have been spared. Yet you and I have crucial knowledge about the death of Christ. If we keep that knowledge to ourselves, some condemned person may die without Christ as his or her Savior.

Be a Lifelong Learner

Many years ago, when adult Training Unions were first being organized, the minister of education at the Broadway Baptist Church in Louisville, Kentucky, announced one Sunday morning that an adult union would be formed that evening. He invited every adult who felt the need for Christian growth and development to be present. At the appointed hour, he waited in the assigned room wondering if any adults would come. Presently he heard footsteps approaching. When the first person to respond entered the room, it was none other than Dr. John R. Sampey, president of the Southern Baptist Theological Seminary.[11] President Sampey was a lifelong learner.

We shall never know everything about faith sharing. The circle of our understanding in evangelism can never be complete, at least not in this life. No matter how much we know about evangelism, we can never know it all. Our own limitations break the circle. Nevertheless, we can and should seek to enlarge that circle.

One of my professional goals is to know everything I can learn about evangelism. I can't know it all, but I can know some of its parts. I can enlarge my circle. Moreover, if I am a faithful steward of that which God gives to me in evangelism, I may even enlarge the corporate circle of the whole people of God.

Nobody can tell you what to say in every situation. We have to learn to depend upon the Holy Spirit to give us what we are to say in times of tension and stress.

One way to be a lifelong learner and to enlarge our circle of knowledge about witnessing is to systematically memorize Scripture. Memorizing Scripture is like putting your money in a credit union. It gives you the capital to do what you need to do when you need to do it. It prepares you for witnessing emergencies. James M. Gray, who was for many years president of Moody Bible Institute, used to say: "Do not ask the Lord to bring back to your mind that which never entered your mind!"[12]

There is a word of exhortation in Hebrews to leave the *ABCs* of Christ and to go on to maturity (see Heb. 6:1). It is time that some of us move on and go forward. We have tarried with our spiritual *ABCs* too long. Maturity and growing up are called for.

Do Not Disdain Small Things

Jim was from India and a tailor in a southern U.S. city. He had been reared in a denomination that had exposed him to the gospel, but no one had ever asked him to receive Christ as his personal Savior and Lord. His wife came from a very different religious background.

One day a former student of mine by the name of Joe went to see Jim about getting a suit made. Inside Joe's coat pocket was a Bible with the Roman road plan of salvation marked out in it. Jim asked Joe what it was he was carrying around. Joe pulled out his Bible and asked if he might share some things with him.

The tailor was most grateful. He got down on his knees and confessed his sins to God. Immediately Jim called his wife and told her he had become a Christian. Joe could tell from the conversation and the expression on Jim's face that his wife was not at all pleased with that news.

Recently, Joe saw his tailor again. Jim was beaming this time. His wife had become a Christian. They were members of a church in Atlanta.

Note that Joe led Jim to Christ through the use of some marked Scriptures called the "Roman road." If you don't know how to lead a lost person to Christ, ask someone who knows the Roman road to show you how to mark these verses in your Bible or New Testament so you'll be able to use them next time you have the opportunity. Something just that simple may be what you need, and what your lost relatives and friends need to enter into the kingdom of God. Let us not disdain such seemingly small things as using a premarked plan of salvation from the Bible.

Some Don'ts in Witnessing

We ought to be hesitant in giving negatives about such a positive ministry as evangelization. Nevertheless, some truths might be garnered by briefly treating some don'ts in evangelism.

A. C. Archibald has suggested that we might share with evangelistic visitors "A Bundle of Don'ts." Several of his more important don'ts are:

• Don't argue. Never argue. You have not the time. Avoid

argument as you would an infection. Out of it only comes bitterness, self-justification, and increased hardness.

- Don't use hackneyed and worn-out phrases. Be natural, your own true self. Don't begin by asking, "Are you saved?" Our Lord never did. Talk in your own everyday language. Some of the most effective witnesses on college campuses are those who became Christians after they got to college. Those witnesses don't have to unlearn a lot of religious language.
- Don't lose your temper. That is fatal. "Keep sweet" is old but good advice.
- Don't get discouraged. Your visit has done good even if your prospect does not accept Christ. You may set in motion a process which will come to fruition years later.[13]

Conclusion

An experienced guide warns us against overtraining gospel reapers. "One can be drilled and instructed until all the bloom of naturalness and simple fervor has been eliminated. The last thing that must appear in any evangelistic worker is artificiality."

That same guide told how he trained his harvesters for two months and then sent them out for their greatest triumph. They had done well the previous year, but this year the additional training would yield even a greater harvest of souls, he thought. Alas! It was their greatest dearth.

They sat down to examine why they had failed so miserably after training so diligently. Finally, one good brother arose and said, "Pastor, I think I know why I failed this year. Last year I went out and tried to be myself, inviting people in just the way I felt like doing. But this year, I have tried to do it like you said, and it dried me up."[14]

Notes

1. Arthur C. Archibald, *New Testament Evangelism* (Philadelphia: The Judson Press, 1946), p. 10.

2. James Armstrong, *From the Underside: Evangelism from a Third World Vantage Point* (Maryknoll, NY: Orbis Books, 1981), p. 2.

3. See Lyle E. Schaller, *Parish Planning* (Nashville: Abingdon Press, 1971), p. 214.

4. See the Associated Press report, "Holiday Became Nightmare for S. C. Man," *Spartanburg Herald*, 31 Dec. 1980, p. B1.

5. See Archibald, *Evangelism*, p. 113.

6. Ibid., pp. 113-114.

7. See ibid., pp. 82-83.

8. Condensed and edited from a true story related by Arthur C. Archibald, ibid., pp. 137-139.

9. Philip Yancey, "Wycliffe: A Mission in Search of a Future," *Christianity Today*, XXVI, No. 4, 19 Feb. 1982, p. 22.

10. Wendell Rawls, Jr., "Witness Comes Forward in 1913 Slaying," *The News and Observer*, 8 Mar. 1982, pp. 1A and 9A.

11. Herschel H. Hobbs, *New Testament Evangelism* (Nashville: Convention Press, 1960), p. 105.

12. Bernard R. De Remer, *Moody Bible Institute: A Pictorial Directory* (Chicago: Moody Press, 1960), p. 50.

13. Selected and adapted from Arthur C. Archibald, *Evangelism*, pp. 106-107.

14. Ibid., p. 89.

8
The Power Barrier

Objection: "I don't have the power to do that!"

Scripture Lesson: Judges 16:4-22; 2 Corinthians 4:7

Introduction

An eighth barrier to witnessing may be called the power barrier. Caught up around the words, "I don't have the power to do that," this obstacle is almost as formidable as that disputed real estate known as Gibraltar.

If you think the "power" question is unimportant, look at the crazy cults on the scene today. "How do I find the power I need to live today?" That's a question persons are asking. All of the talk about healing, do you think it's a farce? Not on your life!

One missiologist categorically says, "Every conversion to Christ . . . is a power confrontation and a power encounter with the totality of humankind in its total life milieu."[1] Every book in the New Testament except Philemon says something about evil spirits. The Bible takes the power question very seriously. If you are unpersuaded, read passages like Ephesians 6:10-17; Acts 1:8; 8:6-24.

While some Christians are bereft of power like Sampson who succumbed to the wiles of Delilah (see Judg. 16:4 *ff.*), most of us probably have more power available to us than we recognize and appropriate. It is true that we have no power in and of ourselves. God is the source of all our witnessing power. His power is greater than any and all powers. There is no power shortage with him who is the Creator, Sustainer, Redeemer, and Sanctifier of the universe. Cryonics notwithstanding, it is appointed to every person once to die and after that the judgment.

None of us can generate the God kind of power. As Paul said: "But we have this treasure in earthen vessels, to show that the transcendent power belongs to God and not to us" (2 Cor. 4:7). But let us consider some of the resources of power which are available to every Christian.

The Power of the Holy Spirit

The power of the Holy Spirit is available to every disciple of Christ. We can overcome the power barrier by asking God to fill us with his Spirit. That Spirit which he has given to us is "a spirit of power" (see 2 Tim. 1:7). Christ promised his disciples, "You shall receive power when the Holy Spirit has come upon you" (Acts 1:8). The word used in Acts 1:8 for "power" is the Greek word from which we get our English word "dynamite."

There is only one baptism with the Holy Spirit. However, there are many fillings and constant anointings with the Spirit. We are filled with the Spirit in the same way that we are saved, namely "by hearing with faith" (see Gal. 3:1-5). Let no one bewitch you into believing that works of the law, even legalistic so-called "spiritual" works, can cause you to be filled with the dynamite of God's Spirit.

Someone asked R. G. LeTourneau, "What do you do if you know the will of God and don't have the faith to act on it?" LeTourneau replied, "If I know the will of God, I just go ahead and act according to it." When that great benefactor died, he left an estate valued in excess of forty million dollars.

We need to talk about the *gift* of faith, but also about the *grace* of faith. The gift of faith is unusual insight, or supernatural insight. There is an emotional element in the grace of faith. Also, there is a volitional element. Action is required. Faith without works is dead.

The basis of faith is truth. You can't just believe anything. You have to believe the truth. And the truth is, "how much more will the heavenly Father give the Holy Spirit to those who ask him!" (Luke 11:13). The truth is, "Ask, and it will be given you" (Luke 11:9).

God gives us his Spirit to empower us for witnessing to him (see Acts 1:8). But the Spirit is also our Paraclete to help us and enable us as we help other weary pilgrims along life's way (see John 14:15-18). Those of us who have experienced the Holy Spirit's advocacy for us are called to be paracletes for others. A paraclete is literally one who is called alongside of another. He or she is an advocate, a helper, one who pleads for another.

We Christians have more than one advocate. Jesus Christ is our Advocate before the Father. Then, we have another Advocate, a kind of second Advocate in the Holy Spirit. Finally, we have our brothers and sisters and other members of God's forever family, the church, to plead for us.

How blessed are we to have so many advocates. Surely you and I, who know the help of so many, are called to be paracletes to the poor and powerless of our world.

The Holy Spirit is also the superintendent of the church. He supplies the church with all the supernatural power she needs to do God's work in the world. Richard G. Hutcheson, Jr., has written a helpful book on the management crisis in the pluralistic church. While Hutcheson affirms the value of MBO (Management by Objectives), OD (Organization Development) and PPBS (Planning, Programming, Budgeting Systems), he contends that the Holy Spirit is really the director of the church. In fact, Hutcheson's book is titled *Wheel Within the Wheel.* It gets its title from the old Negro spiritual which says:

> Ezekiel saw a wheel
> Way up in the middle of the air;
> A Wheel in a wheel,
> Way up in the middle of the air;
> And the big wheel ran by faith,
> And the little wheel ran by the grace
>   of God;
> A wheel in a wheel
> Way up in the middle of the air.

Hutcheson argues that the Holy Spirit is the Wheel within the wheel![2] However many wheels of organization, bureaucrats, and systems there may be, the Holy Spirit is always the Wheel within all the other wheels. If not, the church degenerates into just another social organization.

The Power of a Changed Life

A second resource available to us in overcoming the power barrier is the power of a changed life. One brother described himself as a born-again, Bible-quoting, tongue-talking, water-walking, blood-washed, God-fearing Christian.[3] What else is left to be said? In spite of such inflated and overly pious rhetoric, we can say something about the reality of the transformed life. We Christians were all bloated tadpoles or hairy caterpillars at one time. Now, thank God, we are beautiful butterflies and amphibious bullfrogs as it were. God has so radically changed our nature through conversion that we are no longer what we once were (see Eph. 2:1-10). The old has passed away and all things have become new.

The healing of the nations begins with a healing of ourselves. We cannot be credible witnesses to the Great Physician's power to heal until we have allowed him to heal us.

Conversion is that fundamental change which the Holy Spirit works in the life of a person. It is akin to dying and being raised again from the dead. It is a new birth which brings with it a new mind, a new heart, a new nature, and a new life-style.

Being converted is more than merely joining the church. This transformation implies a change of values, a change in the way one views success, and a change in one's approach to happiness. Professor William B. Coble, a New Testament scholar, says: "True conversion is the point at which one begins turning from man's way of thinking and acting and begins learning to think as God thinks." Coble continues, "Only that kind of change shows that conversion is valid; so it is a drastic experience."[4]

Conversion is not an emotional experience which promises to give a person more peace and potential in pursuing the same old goals of power, success, and wealth. Biblical conversion transforms us as well as satisfies us. It is a God-initiated metamorphosis which gives us power to transform our world.

Senator Hubert Humphrey said in his last speech on Capitol Hill in 1977 that the moral test of government is how we treat those in the dawn of life, our children; those in the twilight of life, our elderly; and those in the shadows of life: the sick, the poor, the needy, and the handicapped. May we not also say that one moral test of those who claim to be under God's government is how the citizens of his Kingdom treat the lost who are outsiders, and in some cases outcasts of society? The life which has been, and is now being changed by the power of God is filled with the power to love God supremely and neighbor as self.

The Power of the Gospel

The power of the gospel also enables us to overcome the power barrier in witnessing. "Humanity today is threatened by raw human nature," said Alan Walker, director of world evangelism for the World Methodist Council. "Unless a power can be tapped which profoundly changes and redeems individual lives, continued Walker, "humanity faces a bleak future."[5] According to the apostle Paul, that power is in the gospel. "For I am not ashamed of the gospel: it is the power of God for salvation to every one who has faith, to the Jew first and also to the Greek" (Rom. 1:16). Paul believed that the righteousness of God is revealed through faith for faith in the gospel (see Rom. 1:17).

The Auca Indians of Ecuador killed five young missionaries in 1956. But they did not kill Christianity. Many volunteered to replace them. And the gospel which they have proclaimed has been God's power to save the Aucas.

Genesis 3:15 has been called the *protoevangelium,* or the first gospel. "I will put enmity . . . / between your seed and her seed; / he shall bruise your head, / and you shall bruise his heel." If those words depict the conflict between Christ and Satan with Christ being victorious, they are the gospel before the Gospels. Moreover, they show the power of the gospel to destroy the seed of the serpent.

When we get to feeling powerless and impotent in the face of our mammoth task of world evangelization, we need to remember that there is enough power in our gospel to save every one who will believe. God has passed down to us through faithful witnesses a constructive power which can liberate the world from its bondage to all the powers of this present and passing age.

The Power of Prayer

Add to the power of the Holy Spirit, the power of a changed life, and the power of the gospel, the power of prayer as another resource available to help us break through the power barrier. An old anonymous couplet says:

Satan trembles when he sees the weakest saint upon his knees.

One of my former students shared with me how God helped him with a dilemma in his life. He was working at a job which he greatly disliked. Work was a drudgery. He had a family to support. His company still had not reimbursed him for a part of the fee which he had paid to find the job which he hated.

Life was a real drag for him. He had stopped praying and had missed going to church for several weeks. Nothing seemed to be going right for him. He was moping around in his apartment wishing in a way that he had never been born. He lay down on the couch feeling sorry for himself and racking his brain to find a way to change his situation.

Then, a line from a gospel song popped into his mind. It spoke of being a person without hope. Said he: "I was convinced that described me to a tee. I just lay there running those words over and over in my mind and feeling so useless and worthless."

But, then, he remembered the next lines of the song which spoke of God reaching down to touch his life. Immediately, like a flash of lightning, he raised up and thought to himself, *You dummy, you've been searching for an answer to your problem from everyone and everything, and you have left Jesus Christ completely out of the process.*

When he put Jesus Christ at the center of the process, he began to pray. It wasn't long before God had completely turned his life around and his dilemma was dissolved.[6]

The Scripture tells us that Jesus "offered up prayers and supplications, with loud cries and tears" (Heb. 5:7). To put the same truth another way, his prayers had pain in them; his supplications contained sobs. "When we cease to bleed, we cease to bless," said J. H. Jowett.

Every Christian witness can find power in importunate and

heartfelt prayer. We may also gain power through prayer partners. Every one who goes out to share his or her faith should be coupled with one or two others who support them in prayer. Long before Evangelism Explosion established a system of prayer partners, A. C. Archibald was using them and even calling them by that designation. "For every team of visitors," said Archibald, "we attach a prayer partner who daily supplicates God for his or her contact partners."7

Archibald knew the power of prayer. James Kennedy and his partners in Evangelism Explosion have also discovered that power. It is available to you and to me as well.

The Power of Persistence

Persistence has a built-in power which may help us overcome the power barrier in faith sharing. Some of us give up on the lost too easily and turn loose of them too quickly. A seventy-eight-year-old man, whom God had mightily used through his church and denomination, told the story of his conversion. He was twenty years old and resistant to all evangelistic efforts. One day a young farmer, keen of mind and wholly devoted, dropped in to see him. He asked straight out, "When all your family have taken their stand, why aren't you a Christian?"

He evaded, but the farmer was persistent. He got a promise that the stubborn young man would at least come to the meeting that night. But he didn't honor his promise and went off somewhere else.

The young farmer was at the young man's gate when he returned home that night. Together they went into the house, up to the young man's room. There they talked, reasoned, and prayed for five hours. At last, at 3:00 AM, the old gentleman said, "I could hold out no longer. The fellow would not let go of my soul." So he said to the farmer, "Well, I give in. I have been wrong. I will accept Christ as my Saviour."

Finally, this elderly gentleman who had served Christ since that long night more than fifty-eight years ago concluded his story by saying: "You know, with the kind of disposition I had, unless God had sent some fellow with just that determined, dogged disposition to hold on to me, I am convinced I never would have been a Christian."[8]

My experience tells me that lay witnesses are more persistent in their witnessing than ordained pastors and evangelists. One Sunday afternoon I went on a witnessing visit with a layman. We found a couple visiting in the kitchen with our prospect. My inclination was to leave and arrange to go back at a more convenient time. The layman would not hear to it. To my surprise, we were graciously welcomed by the prospect. He told us that his visitors were always in and out, and he could see them almost any time. The prospect insisted that we come on in and share with him what was on our minds. There is real power in that kind of faithful persistence.

The Power of Hard Work

There is a word of Scripture to the effect that when Zion travailed she brought forth children (Isa. 66:8). No travail means no new life. The process of the new birth requires some effort and pain. Where there is no cross, there is no salvation. "There never was a bloodless revival," quipped A. C. Archibald. He knew very well that evangelism was hard work. "It is such a difficult and soul-burdening task that it demands the last ounce of sacrificially consecrated energy of the Christian believer," said he.[9]

The work of evangelism, if effective, wrote Archibald is "a very disturbing thing." He continued:

> It drains our strength and time and ability. It demands a place of undisputed primacy in our affections and devotions, or it will not live with us at all. Therefore, the followers of the "cult of the comfortable" dislike evangelism.[10]

John Mbiti, an African scholar from Kenya and Uganda, has explained the growth of the church in Africa this way, "Man's evangelism has two dimensions: the human effort and the divine superintendence."[11] There is power in honest human effort. We can with God's help turn the world upside down and lives right side up! God has given us power to raise the dead—those who are dead in trespasses and sins. But witnessing is too energetic for lazy persons.

When H. Leo Eddleman was a pastor, he made every effort to visit frequently. One afternoon in his ten-year pastorate he made seventeen visits. An insurance executive heard about it and invited him to lunch. The executive asked Eddleman if it was true that he had made seventeen visits in one afternoon. Eddleman replied, "Yes, but five of them were not in." The executive right on the spot invited Eddleman to join his company with over twice the salary he was then making and with a promise of much more.[12] The business world certainly recognizes the power of hard work. If we will combine our diligent human efforts with divine superintendence, we can overcome the power barrier.

Neither the natural birth or the spiritual birth can be fully explained. There is an element of mystery and miracle about both of them. We can only cooperate with God to bring either about. When we cooperate with God by doing our part both in physical and spiritual birth, the miracle of new life is the result.

Conclusion

God has given to us Christians the power of "the keys of the kingdom of heaven" (see Matt. 16:19). We may not be able to evangelize the whole world, but we can seek to evangelize our areas of influence. We can do our part in our church and community. One man with a speech impediment won over one hundred persons to Christ in six different revival meetings. If such a handicapped person could be so effective in overcoming the power barrier, how much more should those of us who have no such hinderances triumph?

"Now to him who by the power at work within us is able to do far more abundantly than all that we ask or think, to him be glory in the church and in Christ Jesus to all generations, for ever and ever. Amen" (Eph. 3:20-21).

Notes

1. George W. Peters, *A Theology of Church Growth* (Grand Rapids, MI: Zondervan Publishing House, 1981), p. 201.

2. See Richard G. Hutcheson, Jr., *Wheel Within the Wheel: Confronting the Management Crisis of the Pluralistic Church* (Atlanta: John Knox Press, 1979).

3. See the letters to the editor, *Christianity Today*, XXV, No. 17, 2 Oct. 1981, pp. 10 and 105.

4. William B. Coble, "True Conversion Involves Total Submission to Christ," *Word and Way*, 119, No. 2, 14 Jan. 1982, p. 8.

5. See "Walker Stresses Personal Conversion," *World Evangelization*, Information Bulletin No. 26, March 1982, p. 10.

6. Related by Ralph Brown in an unpublished paper for my M4500, Basic Evangelism, in the fall of 1981 at Southeastern Baptist Theological Seminary. The paper is entitled "My Life Story as It Relates to the Gospel Story." See especially pp. 7-8.

7. Arthur C. Archibald, *New Testament Evangelism* (Philadelphia: The Judson Press, 1946), p. 82.

8. Ibid., pp. 142-43.

9. Ibid., p. 56.

10. Ibid., p. 55.

11. James Armstrong, *From the Underside: Evangelism from a Third World Vantage Point* (Maryknoll, NY: Orbis Books, 1981), p. 43.

12. See the chapter by H. Leo Eddleman in *If I Had My Ministry to Live Over, I Would . . .* Rick Ingle, compiler, (Nashville: Broadman Press, 1977), p. 40.

9
The Theological Barrier

Objection: "I don't believe . . ."

Scripture Lesson: Psalms 138:1-8; Matthew 14:22-36

Introduction

We come now to the theological barrier. The objection begins, "I don't believe, . . ." and is completed with a wide variety of statements. Examples of this barrier are: "I don't believe persons are really lost"; "I don't believe in a real hell"; "I don't believe we should be aggressive in evangelizing"; and "I don't believe we should bother with that person because he has blasphemed the Holy Spirit." The list goes on and on, almost endlessly. Let us deal honestly and candidly with some of these objections which constitute a theological barrier to faith sharing.

The Lost

First, let's look at that objection which says, "I don't believe persons are really lost." Pastor Martin Niemöeller, that stalwart Christian who opposed Hitler so vigorously, once summed up Christian ethics in the question: "What would Jesus say?" That question first caught his attention as an eight-year-old schoolboy.[1] A large part of our theological problem in evangelism is that we see ourselves in the judge's seat rather than on the witness stand.

Jesus was the one who told the stories about the lost sheep, the lost coin, and the lost son (see Luke 15). Persons who are not citizens of God's kingdom are as lost as was the lost sheep, the lost coin, and the lost prodigal. They are in great peril and imminent danger (see Luke 15:3-7). They are incomplete and failing to fulfill their created purpose (see Luke 15:8-10). They are separated from the Father, depraved and in a state of death (see Luke 15:11-32). According to John's Gospel, Jesus did not come to condemn the

world, but those who do not believe in the Son are already condemned (see John 3:16-21). They are now under the wrath of God
(see John 3:36). They will die in their sins unless they believe in
Jesus as the light of the world (see John 8:24). Those who do not
believe that Jesus came from the Father are children of the devil
(see John 8:44). Jesus himself said, "He who is not with me is
against me, and he who does not gather with me scatters" (Matt.
12:30).

Paul, who knew the mind of Christ so well, told us that all are
"under the power of sin" (Rom. 3:9). The lost are in a state of death
(see Eph. 2:1-5). They are "by nature children of wrath" (Eph. 2:3),
"separated from Christ" (Eph. 2:12), without hope "and without
God in the world" (Eph. 2:12). Furthermore, Paul concluded that
all unreconciled persons are enemies of God (Rom. 5:10) and are
spiritually blind (2 Cor. 4:3-4).

Somerset Maugham wrote of an old couple in *Of Human Bondage,* "It was as if they had never lived at all." So far as the kingdom
of God is concerned, that may be said of all who never receive the
gift of eternal life.

One thing which makes the gospel such good news is that it is
the opposite of the bad news about sin, judgment, and hell. The
world has a large supply of beautiful faces, beautiful figures,
beautiful hairstyles, and beautiful clothes. But there is a scarcity
of beautiful feet. Whether you and I believe that persons without
Jesus Christ as their Lord and Savior are lost or not doesn't change
the fact that Jesus said they are lost.

Seeking and Saving the Lost

Second, closely allied with the objection that persons are not
really lost is the belief that even if they are, we don't need to do
anything to seek or save them. Often this objector will say, "I don't
believe there is anything we should do to seek or save the lost."

In 1946, A. C. Archibald called our attention to the erosion of
intentionality in evangelism: "The modern Christian has largely
ceased to be a propagandist of his faith. He is even suspicious that
to attempt to change another man's conviction, in the realm of
religion, may partake of the spirit of impertinence."[2]

The Bible, however, from Genesis to Revelation presents God

as a seeking God. Genesis tells us how God came down and sought after Adam, saying, "Where are you?" (Gen. 3:9). Then, in the last book of the Bible we hear the Lord saying, "Behold, I stand at the door and knock; if anyone hears my voice and opens the door, I will come in to him and eat with him, and he with me" (Rev. 3:20). Jesus himself said, "For the Son of man came to seek and to save the lost" (Luke 19:10). If we pattern our evangelizing after Jesus the perfect model evangelist and do for others what God has done for us, we shall also seek after the lost of our world in order that God may save them too. It is this "seeking" element which we need so much to recover in our evangelism.

Seeking to Convert

Third, some will further object, "I don't believe we should try to convert persons to our point of view." Can you imagine Marxists following that line of logic? Karl Marx said in his commentary on Feuerback: "The philosophers have only interpreted the world, in various ways; the point, however, is to *change* it." Marxism has done much to change the world. My personal opinion is that much of that change has been evil rather than good. Nevertheless, I think we Christians would do well to heed the point made by Marx. Our mission is to change the world, to turn it right side up, and not simply to interpret it.

We Christians are God's change agents. We deal first of all with that most profound of all changes, what the Bible calls repentance. No other change is so revolutionary, so total, and so liberating as biblical repentance. Repentance is a complete about-face. It is a change from the inside out which seeks to conform one to the image of Christ. No wonder the Bible teaches that such a change makes one a new creation, gives one a new heart, and brings with it a new set of Kingdom values.

The true Marxists will not agree that they should not try to make converts to their point of view. Nor will the militant Muslims. The number of Muslims now almost equals the number of nominal Christians in the world. Soon, one of every four persons in the world will be a Muslim. In 1900 the Muslim population was estimated at 100 million as compared to 500 million Christians. Islam now claims about 700 million adherents worldwide as compared to perhaps one billion Christians. Eberhard Troeger, director of the Protestant Mission in Upper Egypt, has pointed out that both reform and conservative wings of Islam view their religion as the great alternative to the materialistic West and the atheistic East.[3]

Our nation's first all-Muslim community is now being built near Abriquiu, New Mexico. A projected 600-member settlement is the goal. Most of these are American converts.[4]

Intrinsic to the Christian faith is a desire to make converts to Jesus Christ as Lord. Karl Rahner has pictured devout persons of non-Christian religions as "anonymous Christians." I agree with John Hick's assessment that such a characterization "is too manifestly an ad hoc contrivance to satisfy many. For it is as easy, and as arbitrary, to label devout Christians as anonymous Muslims, or anonymous Hindus, as to label devout Hindus or Muslims as anonymous Christians."[5] Such labels may also turn out to be nothing more than new terms for the old heresy of universalism—the teaching that all persons are saved whether they acknowledge and openly confess Christ or not.

Missionary surgeon Don Duvall is an example of the kind of Christian witnesses which we need to represent Christ in our world. Duvall works a hectic schedule at Kedari Baptist Hospital in Indonesia. He says the end of his work is not to practice the highest medicine available but to practice in such a way that the gospel is spread. It is that strong sense of mission which has taken Duvall and his physician wife to a far away country and cut them off from lucrative practices in Kentucky.[6]

We need to seek to convert persons with the same attitude which the great Puritan preacher Richard Baxter exhibited when he said:

> I preached as never sure to preach again,
> And as a dying man to dying men.[7]

Hell

A fourth theological barrier which is often thrown up against witnessing goes something like this, "I don't believe there is a real hell." A recent survey of Canadians revealed that less than half of

the members of the United Church of Canada profess an un-
equivocal belief in God.⁸ If Christians don't believe in God, we
should not be surprised that they don't believe in hell. My experience has taught me that what one believes about God ultimately
determines what he or she believes about almost everything else.

You may believe like the Jehovah's Witnesses that the only hell
is the grave. One person said, "I believe hell is my mother-in-law."
But I must tell you that at the end of every lost person's life is a
place called hell.

A favorite aphorism of Martin Luther King, Jr. was, "Hell is
when the Lord gives you what you thought you wanted." God is
indeed merciful in not always giving us what we want. He knows
what we need better than do we. Nevertheless, the essence of hell
seems to be separation from God.

The story about the rich man and Lazarus indicates that "a great
chasm has been fixed" between hades and "Abraham's bosom," or
the place where the rich man was and that other place where
Lazarus was. The separation was permanent, and the rich man in
hades did not want to see his five brothers come there. And yet
the place of torment and separation was the place where persons went who did not hear Moses and the prophets (see Luke
16:19-31).

I do not believe God sends persons to hell. They send themselves there because of their unbelief and hardness of heart. God
had never stopped loving that rich man. Even though he was in
hades, God loved him still. Notice that Abraham called him "Son"
(see Luke 16:25). That's the voice of love, the voice of a broken
heart. The trouble was the rich man had refused to hear Moses and
the prophets in his earthly life. And it was too late for him to start
hearing the law and the prophets in the life beyond this life. We
have no reason to suppose that even death itself will change the
character and conduct of the selfish persons of this world, of which
the rich man is exhibit A. When the rich man cried out, "Father
Abraham, send Lazarus," he was still wanting to use Lazarus.

"Hear" is a key word in Luke sixteen (see Luke 16:31). "See" is
a key word in the judgment scene of Matthew 25. We are judged
on the basis of our hearing and seeing. Hell awaits all who will not
hear the Word of the Lord and who will not see Christ in their

needy brothers and sisters (see both Luke 16:19-31 and Matt.
25:31-46).

A gentleman whom I know once had an engagement scheduled
for Sioux Falls, South Dakota. His flight was to get him there thirty
minutes prior to his engagement. He had excellent connections
and arrived right on schedule. The only trouble was that he
arrived in Sioux City, Iowa, instead of Sioux Falls, South Dakota.
He had failed to check his ticket and assumed his secretary had
everything in order. What a surprise!

How many persons have thought they were going one place and
ended up in another. That was true of certain persons in the
judgment scene of Matthew 25. It was true of the man who was
broke and without a job who said, "Ten years earlier I thought I
was on my way to the top of the company." It was true of the
recently separated couple who said, "We thought we were going
to live happily ever after." We don't always get to where we think
we are going. Check your itinerary carefully before it is too late.

The Necessity of Conversion

Some Christians are bold to say, "I don't believe in the necessity
of conversion." That is a fifth objection which constitutes the theological barrier. Persons do need education. But more than that
they need conversion. A just society will come about through the
concerned labors of just men and women. Freedom in a society
requires that persons be free within.

California has experimented with self-service gas stations. You
don't need any cash. A red, white, and blue debit card inserted
into a computer terminal near the gas pump will do. Isn't that the
ultimate in self-service?[9] No, the ultimate in self-service is trying
to convert yourself. Only the Son of God can set us free from
bondage to sin and all other bondages. "So if the Son makes you
free, you will be free indeed" (John 8:36). Jesus said, "Unless you
turn and become like children, you will never enter the kingdom
of heaven" (Matt. 18:3).

The church always has an unfinished evangelistic responsibility
to the younger generation. Nobody is born a Christian. Even if you
believe in infant baptism as do many denominations, you still need
to believe in the necessity of conversion. "The assumption that

children born within the Christian fellowship will be good Christians," said Anglican Bishop Stephen Neill, "is what has largely undercut the whole of our Christian witness."[10]

Margaret Sangster, the great social worker, once related the story of her ministry in the slums of a large city. She had arranged for a gymnasium to be open to boys in the neighborhood after school. One afternoon a lad hobbled into the gym on crutches. One of his legs was twisted badly and turned backwards. In conversation Miss Sangster discovered that the boy had been hit by a truck.

The compassionate social worker had the boy examined by an orthopedic surgeon. There seemed to be no medical reason why a series of operations would not restore the lad's ability to walk normally. Miss Sangster got the doctors to agree to perform the surgery without pay, and a bank president and some of his friends agreed to pay the hospital bill. The boy's parents gave their consent for the surgery.

A series of intricate operations were performed. Then followed weeks of therapy. Finally the day came when that boy walked into the gym, ran down the court, and sent a basketball spinning through the net. Margaret Sangster said, "When I saw that boy run, I shed tears of joy!"

Then Miss Sangster paused and asked her audience: "That boy is now grown, and do you know what he is doing today? No, he is not serving as a preacher, judge, doctor, or educator. No, he is not a schoolteacher, a farmer, or a blue collar worker. He is serving three life sentences in the penitentiary for robbery and murder."

Then with tears streaming down her cheeks, Margaret Sangster said, "I was so busy teaching that boy *how* to walk that I forgot to teach him *where* to walk!"

Our children need to be converted to Christ. So does every person on this planet. Those who don't believe in conversion are the ones who need it most.

The testimony of those who have become Christians often refutes those who say they don't believe in the necessity of conversion. Wei Wen-long, a college student in the People's Republic of China who became a Christian, gave this testimony:

Since I became a Christian I seem to have become another man.
My life becomes brighter and fresher. My heart is always overflow-
ing with a new feeling of happiness. I have become more energetic
and confident. Everything I do, I do with eagerness.[11]

Blasphemy Against the Spirit

Some Christians have been heard to say, "I don't believe we
should bother with that person because he has blasphemed the
Holy Spirit." This is a sixth objection which a few well-meaning
witnesses will lift up.

"The sin against the Holy Spirit is one of the greatest obstacles
encountered by the soul-winner," wrote Herschel H. Hobbs.
"Thinking that he has committed this sin, a person does not try to
believe in Jesus. But such a feeling is proof that he has not so
sinned. For his consciousness of sin proves that the Holy Spirit is
still striving with him."[12]

Now, if we add to that obstacle mentioned by Hobbs the barrier
which exists in the witness, we do face a formidable foe in reaching
such persons. I seriously doubt that we should ever assume any
person is guilty of the unpardonable sin. Who are we to make such
a weighty judgment? Have we pondered the consequences of such
a presumption?

I believe blasphemy against the Holy Spirit is attributing to the
devil the work of God and to God the work of the devil (see Mark
3:28-30). There is no forgiveness for this sin because those who
commit it are conscious of no sin or need for forgiveness. We
should also make large allowances at this point for possible mental
illness. Up to this point in my life, so far as I know, I have never
met a person who has committed this sin. Have you?

False Doctrine of Election

A seventh objection is raised by those who say, "I believe certain
persons are predestined to heaven and certain others are predestined to hell, and there is nothing we can or should do about it."

Some falsely interpret the doctrine of election to mean that the
sovereign God has elected some to be saved, while all others are
elected to be lost. Such an attitude overemphasizes the sovereign
will of God to the neglect of the free will of persons. It minimizes

God's righteousness and love while magnifying his will and power. It results in an attitude of fatalism.

"This attitude is devastating in the area of evangelism," says Herschel H. Hobbs. "If some men are elected to salvation, and others are elected to damnation, with no consideration of man's free choice, why try to evangelize them at all?" Moreover, why should persons be concerned about their own salvation, if it has already been determined by God?[13]

Evangelist Dwight L. Moody reportedly said to those who were afraid of offending God with their doctrine of man's responsibility toward his own salvation: "Preach the gospel to all; and if you convert anyone who was not chosen, God will forgive you." I recommend that advice to those who are hung up on "double-edged" predestination.

Conclusion

One pastor suggested that ecclesiastical laziness is more of a threat to us Christians than theological liberalism. I suspect that is true of many churches in America.

I heard President Randall Lolley of Southeastern Baptist Theological Seminary tell about a Texas rancher who bought ten ranches and put them all together into one big spread. Someone asked him the name of his new ranch. The Texan replied: "It's the Circle Q, Rambling Brook, Double Bar, Broken Circle, Crooked Creek, Golden Horseshoe, Lazy B, Bent Arrow, Sleepy T, Triple O Ranch."

"Wow!" the inquirer said, "I bet you have a lot of cattle."

"Nope," said the Texan.

"Why not?"

"Not many survive the branding," the rancher explained.

We can get so hung up on branding ourselves and others with what we don't believe and with what we must believe that unbelievers will perish in their sins while we kill ourselves and them with our theological branding. Kierkegaard spoke of "the sickness unto death." I don't know if this theological barrier is the sickness unto death, but it does have some consequences which may be fatal. Karl Barth may have been right in that famous line of his which says, "Religion is unbelief."

And yet, we need to admit that some Christians are hung up on how little they can believe and still call themselves Christians. I believe there are certain theological convictions which will help us to be effective in our witnessing. A highly successful pastor, who had trained lay evangelists for thirty-five years, said there are five basic assumptions one must build upon if he or she is to succeed in evangelism:

- All persons need a Savior, and that Savior is here with us.
- God's chief agency in reaching lost persons is other persons.
- We can always presume that God, the Holy Spirit, is at work when we are at work. This is his task before it is ours.
- Our chief equipment in influencing lost persons is not our talent or influence but our spirit of concern.
- There are always some lost persons who are ready to respond to our invitation. They have been made ready by God's Spirit and are waiting our coming. It never fails.[14]

Notes

1. See the editorial interview with Martin Niemöeller, "What Would Jesus Say?" *Sojourners,* 10, No. 8 (Aug. 1981), p. 14.

2. Arthur C. Archibald, *New Testament Evangelism* (Philadelphia: The Judson Press, 1946), p. 55.

3. See "Christian Leader Cites Muslim Expansion," *World Evangelization,* Information Bulletin No. 26, March 1982, p. 11.

4. See *Christianity Today,* XXV, No. 12, 26 June 1981, p. 35.

5. John Hick, "Pluralism and the Reality of the Transcendent," *The Christian Century,* XCVIII, No. 2, 21 Jan. 1981, p. 48.

6. See the BP release, "Surgeon in Indonesia Says Evangelism Is Main Purpose," *The Baptist Courier,* 113, No. 26, 25 June 1981, p. 9.

7. Herschel H. Hobbs, *New Testament Evangelism* (Nashville: Convention Press, 1960), p. 66.

8. Leslie K. Tarr, "The Incredible State of Canada's Largest Protestant Denomination," *Christianity Today,* XXVI, No. 4, 19 Feb. 1982, p. 28.

9. See the UPI report, "Calif. Checks Out Computerized Gasoline Stations," *The News and Observer,* 10 Feb. 1982, p. 1A.

10. See the interview with Stephen Neill, "Building the Church on Two Continents," *Christianity Today,* XXIV, No. 14, 18 July 1980, p. 22.

11. Wei Wen-long, "I Am Happy, I Have Become Another Man," *Decision*, 23, No. 4 (April 1982), p. 3.

12. Hobbs, *Evangelism*, p. 38.

13. *Ibid.*, pp. 23-24.

14. Adapted from Archibald, *Evangelism*, p. 90.

10
The Stranger Barrier

Objection: "You can't witness to total strangers."

Scripture Lesson: Ruth 1:15-18; Acts 8:26-40

Introduction

You are no stranger to the stranger barrier if you have ever heard a Christian say, "You can't witness to total strangers." Variations of this objection may be: "I don't know him well enough to talk to him about Christ"; "Witnessing is too personal a matter to share with folk whom we hardly know"; "I barely know that individual, and you mean you want me to confront him with the claims of God upon his life?"

Bridging the Credibility Gap

A preliminary answer to this objection is a partial agreement. It is more difficult to witness to total strangers than to persons with whom we have meaningful relationships. Relational evangelism is the best kind. Friendship evangelism is superior to "cold turkey" evangelism.

Before some persons will hear us on a subject as personal as faith in Christ, we may have to earn a right to be heard by them. This was brought home to me with renewed force in 1981. I was in York, Pennsylvania, leading some Bible studies for a state conference on evangelism. One of the pastors said to me on the second day, "You established your credibility with me yesterday when you shared your testimony with us." He went on to observe, "I don't like to be hollered at and made to feel any more guilty than I already feel when I come to a meeting like this."

My conversation with this pastor took place immediately following the third of four powerful messages by one of the outstanding preachers in America. Yet, the young pastor said to me with a great deal of feeling, "Dr. So and So has just now established his credibility with me; up until a few minutes ago I didn't know from where he was coming!"

Credibility: how important it is in a preacher, a witness, a leader. Some persons never really hear us or believe us until we establish our credibility with them. That may be just another way of saying we do have to earn the right to be heard. Perhaps we would do well to reflect upon how we can more quickly bridge the credibility gap in our preaching and teaching and witnessing.

Therefore, there is some truth in the objection, "You can't witness to total strangers." But you can become friends with total strangers, win their confidence, then share with them the most precious treasure you have—your faith. Wanda Barker, for example, met Diane Edwards in a course on group dynamics at the community college near Annapolis, Maryland. They were total strangers to each other. Barker was a fifty-year-old grandmother, and Edwards was a twenty-year-old with dark hair and flaming eyes. Barker was a warm, loving Christian. Edwards was somewhere between being an agnostic and an atheist.

These fellow students were assigned to the same group to learn how to be open and how to lead a small group. Somebody in the group asked Barker how she managed to be friendly all the time. Almost bashfully, she responded: "You don't want to hear this, but it's because I've got Jesus Christ." Then, she proceeded to share her testimony.

That turned Edwards off. Yet, despite their differences in age and faith, the two became fast friends. Edwards attended a renewal consultation with Barker, ostensibly to view Barker's leadership capabilities. Barker began inviting Edwards to dinner on weekends and to church, where Edwards attended the college age Sunday School class. But it was the dinners and the talks afterwards which got to Edwards.

Barker would say, "Let's go into the living room and sit down and talk." Many times Edwards wound up spending the night. Barker treated her like a member of the family. They talked through Edwards's reasons for rejecting Christ. After several months of friendship with Barker, Edwards accepted Christ as her Lord and Savior.[1] I think that is a beautiful example of how one faithful Christian witness overcame the stranger barrier in witnessing. Barker, in fact not only won one who at first was a total stranger; she remarkably overcame the generation gap as well.

Several ways, therefore, to win strangers is to tell them who we are in relationship to Christ, be friendly toward them, practice hospitality, invite them into our churches and homes, and freely enter into honest conversation with them. The stranger barrier can often be overcome through genuine friendship and the practice of Christian hospitality.

Lonely People

If we would overcome this stranger barrier, it may help us to recall how lonely many persons are in our society. One fifth of the American population now lives alone. That of course does not automatically mean they are lonely. But one study found that, regardless of age, relatively isolated persons had a mortality rate of 2.5 times higher than persons with strong social bonds which researchers defined as any combination of marriage, friends, church, and informal club affiliations. As many as 85 percent of men said they have no intimate friends. Furthermore, fears of homosexuality and lesbianism apparently inhibit intimate friendships in our culture.[2]

Do you know just how desperate some persons are to talk to anyone who will listen to them? So desperate that a millwright named Al has set up a conversation center on a dark side street in Spokane, Washington. The center is named Let's Talk and is staffed by Al himself and two ladies who work on commission. For $15.00 Al or one of his staff members will listen to anyone talk about anything for thirty minutes. If a half hour won't do it, you can buy one hour for $25.00.

Let's Talk is no farce. It averages two customers a day.[3] Who knows, perhaps Al will franchise his conversation centers. I see this as a realistic version of Taylor Caldwell's novel, *The Listener.*

On a Tuesday night in 1982 I went with a visitation team of two ladies from our congregation to call on a young mother who had visited our church the previous Sunday night. She lived in a mobile home park about four or five miles distance from the church building. We had some difficulty locating her. But when we arrived, she graciously welcomed us and introduced us to her four-year-old daughter. This beautiful lady was a divorcee; I estimated her to be about twenty-five years of age. She lived all alone with her daughter, had no relatives closer than Indiana, was unemployed, and had no support network of friends in her new community. She told us several times how lonely she was and how grateful for our visit.

We Christians, who once were strangers to God and to God's people, should of all persons on the earth know the importance of welcoming strangers, visiting the lonely, and listening to lonely voices. Has not God said: "Do not neglect to show hospitality to strangers, for thereby some have entertained angels unawares" (Heb. 13:2)?

Strangers on the Earth

First Peter is addressed to certain scattered "strangers" (see 1 Pet. 1:1, KJV). One of our problems in witnessing may be that we think of ourselves as scattered strangers on the earth. Thinking of ourselves as strangers wherever we happen to be can work against witnessing in at least three aspects.

The New Testament calls the Christians followers of "the Way" (see Acts 9:2). Those who follow Christ are essentially travelers. We are a pilgrim people. This world is not our permanent home. We can get so caught up in the thoughts of going to heaven ourselves that we may forget those who are unregenerate. That's one way in which the scattered stranger idea can be twisted to hinder witnessing.

A false sense of place and an illusion about time are two other aspects of the stranger idea which keeps some of us from actively and aggressively bearing witness to Jesus Christ wherever and whenever we are. Like ancient Israel during the Babylonian captivity, we cry out, "How shall we sing the Lord's song in a foreign land?" (Ps. 137:4). We tend to think that we can't witness except "back home" or until we finish our interim assignment, whatever that may be.

Some of us spend so much time and energy living where we aren't that we don't notice the blessings of God where we are. It is difficult for us to break our ties with home and hearth even for a few days. Do you remember talking for days about nothing but getting away? You wanted to go to a place where there were no phones, just peace and quiet for a restful vacation. Then, the first day of your vacation you wanted change to buy the hometown newspaper.

The late Carlyle Marney said, "So much of life is spent in the meantime." Most of us are waiting ones. Almost everybody is waiting for something. Jeremiah told us how to live life in the meantime. He admonished us to live where we are (see Jer. 29:5-6). We have to realize that life is made up of little things. Also, we are to live life in the meantime by seeking the welfare of the city where God has sent us (see Jer. 29:7).

Wars, technology, economics, politics, famines and other natural disasters have made permanent exiles out of many of us, Christians and non-Christians alike. If we postpone singing the Lord's song until we are again in some familiar place or some bygone time, we shall never overcome the stranger barrier in world evangelization.

There is a tree which grows above the "tree line" high in the Andes. It is the eucalyptus with its rough, peeling, multicolored bark. One may find the eucalyptus as high as 11,000 feet. Usually they grow together in clusters to sustain and protect each other. Originally they were imported from Australia.

You may think you can't survive, let alone thrive, in some strange environment. Yet God may surprise you by letting you take root in unexpected places. Especially can you do it if you cluster together with other Christians so that you can sustain and guard each other.

Persistence in Proclamation

Persistence in the proclamation of the gospel by rank-and-file members of the Christian community to complete strangers does produce converts to Christ and his church. John F. Havlik, a first generation American whose parents immigrated to the United States from Austria-Hungary, has told how his family moved during the Great Depression from Milwaukee, Wisconsin, to Tulsa, Oklahoma. Havlik, his sisters, and parents were nominal Catholics. Through the loving, caring ministry of Southern Baptists Havlik and his two sisters became born-again Christians and eventually Southern Baptists. However, when Southern Baptists visited the Havlik home, John's mother would say, "We are Catholics" or "We are Lutherans" (depending upon which she thought would frighten them the most). Those Southern Baptists were not frightened. They kept coming back even when the door had been slammed in their faces. They asked, "Do you ever go to church?" Then, they asked, "Have you been born again?" Such persistent questions finally led three persons into the kingdom of God.[4]

Eugene Skelton's historical novel on Shubal Stearns and the Separate Baptists has Jeremiah Boatwright say to Nancy Kitrell at one point long before his conversion:

> Just about everyone I speak to seems to want to talk about him [Shubal Stearns]. I get thrown in gaol and the galor talks about the New Lights. I look out my window and hear one of them telling about his experience behind a loom. I meet your Uncle John and he passed me on to his friend Ben Merrill who can hardly wait to show me the road to the New Light Meeting House. Someone points a gun at me and tells me about the Baptist meetings. I offer a tanner a place to live and discover he must be off to hear Stearns speak. And when I ride with the prettiest girl in all the province she talks about going to meetings.[5]

That's the kind of gospel presence and proclamation which enabled Elder Shubal Stearns to baptize about eight hundred converts during his first year as pastor of Sandy Creek Baptist Church, and to have a membership of over six hundred by the end of the second year.[6]

Our wayside witnessing can occur anywhere: in the office, on the street, on the golf course, on the tennis court, everywhere. It can happen to a Virginian like Jeremiah Boatwright while in exile to North Carolina. And it can be done by a Christian Jeremiah Boatwright while traveling and sojourning anywhere on the face of the Lord's good earth.

Both saturation and confrontation are needed to bring persons to Jesus. Saturation without confrontation is incomplete. By the same token, confrontation without saturation is incomplete.

Availability to God

Our availability to be used of God may be the missing ingredient in confronting some strangers to the saving grace of God in Christ. Consider the availability of Philip who witnessed to a stranger on the road from Jerusalem to Gaza (see Acts 8:26-40). Philip certainly didn't know the Ethiopian eunuch.

My guess is that the angel of the Lord instructed him to make this witnessing encounter in answer to someone's prayers. Nothing lies beyond the reach of prayer, except that which lies beyond the will of God. The Holy Spirit, who superintends all witnessing, said to Philip: "Go up and join this chariot" (Acts 8:29).

Note that as Philip made himself available to the Lord, God made Philip available to a stranger on a desert road. He provided the opportunity, the prospect, and the very Scripture text which Philip used to lead this stranger into the Kingdom. May we not conclude that when willing witnesses make themselves available to be used by God, he in turn makes available to them whatever is necessary for effective evangelization?

Laura Fry Allen has shared with us one of the most remarkable examples I have heard on how God used a Christian lady to lead an obscene phone caller to faith in Christ. Georgiana had been a Christian for about five years. She had been focusing on making herself available to be used in witnessing experiences. On that unforgettable day, she had to leave work to take her sick little boy home from school.

Georgiana said to the Lord as she entered her house, "Lord, I'm available. If you want me to share with someone whom you may bring to my door or over the phone, I'm available." So about ten minutes later when her phone rang, she was prepared to share her witness to Christ. Imagine her surprise when she heard an obscene caller on the other end of her line. He went through his spiel saying some lewd things and asked her some questions.

Instead of hanging up, Georgiana said: "You've asked me some questions, may I ask you something?" "Sure, lady," the caller replied. Then she said: "It's obvious you're looking for some form of love, right?" He answered: "Well, you could say that, lady."

"Well," said Georgiana, "I can introduce you to someone who

can love you in a way you've never been loved before." The man said, "Lady, what are you talking about?"

Right then and there this willing witness began to share Christ with the man over the phone. He listened intently but couldn't believe what he was hearing. Finally, he said, "Lady, are there more people in the world like you?" Georgiana joyfully said, "Yes, down on the corner of 28th and Sheridan there is a whole church full of us."

"I'd like to meet a group like that," said he. Georgiana made an appointment to meet him with her husband in the lobby of the church on the next Sunday morning at ten minutes before the worship service. Later, the caller told her that he had never heard the gospel. Following three weeks of constant church attendance, a new citizen was born into the kingdom of God.

Today, that converted obscene telephone caller is one of the leading deacons in his church. He doesn't talk so much about his past in sharing his testimony. Instead, he dwells on what Christ means to him right now.[7] Georgiana had every right to refuse to talk to that once-obscene stranger. Instead, she took him alive for Jesus Christ (see Luke 5:10).

Switch Throwing

We should be willing to begin with strangers wherever they are. Some of them are very far from God whereas others are just outside the door of the Kingdom. Leighton Ford sees the evangelist as a switch thrower. Through the wisdom of God and the illumination of his Spirit we have to, in season and out of season, seek to flip the switch which will turn the lost into the paths of light.

A young man entered the New York subway car on which there was a group of Southern Baptist mission directors. It was a chilly spring night and the mission directors were huddled in their overcoats. The young man's feet were bare, scratched and scarred from the pavement, and missing one toe. One of the mission directors impulsively sat down beside the youth, removed his own shoes and socks and gave them to him. Later, one of them said that was "the strongest sermon I've seen this year."[8]

I would say the mission director was trying to throw the switch which would illuminate and warm and capture that young man for life. He went so far as to give his own shoes and socks to a total stranger. *Agapē* love leads us to do some strange things. It is love in action. Sometimes it acts impulsively and spontaneously toward total strangers like that.

Carl Nelson was five years old when he started hating white people. Innocently he stepped into a public wading pool occupied by a white child. That was in Mississippi in the late 1950s. The white child's mother sent an older, bigger brother to beat Carl up. Nelson recalled twenty-two years later: "That's when I started hating both white people and God. How could God allow that boy to beat me up?"

Nelson kept on hating whites until at age seventeen he was converted to Jesus Christ. He heard a preacher tell how Jesus was beaten and persecuted, yet he prayed, "Father, forgive them." The preacher threw the switch. That made him want to read more about Jesus. It sent him to the Bible. Today, Carl Nelson is preaching the gospel and going to seminary. He feels the Lord is leading him to preach the gospel to the poor and to the "put-down" in both black and white ghettos. God has shown him that there is not a separate gospel for blacks and whites.[9]

All it takes to turn some strangers to God is a willing, loving witness who will throw the right switch for that individual. For some the proper switch has to be deeds of love, mercy, and justice along with words. For others a perfect model like Jesus will suffice. Whatever switch we attempt to turn on, we need to remember that we don't use "churchese" to communicate with the world. To do that we speak "worldese." That is to say, we can't communicate with strangers in a language foreign to them.

The Use of Humor

May I be so bold as to suggest that humor is frequently a language common to strangers? Politicians use it all the time. Why can't Christian witnesses learn from them?

Sam J. Ervin, a former United States senator from North Carolina, used humor very effectively in his political career. Senator Ervin believes that humor at its best is perceiving wisdom and communicating it in comical ways that command attention. He sees humor as the only convincing evidence that humankind has superiority over the other creatures of the earth. Apparently except for the so-called laughing hyena, the Creator denied all other creatures the capacity to laugh.

One thing discovered about humor by Ervin is that persons don't plan to be humorous. He found that humor is normally spontaneous. A client, for ex. mple, visited his law office and wanted a divorce from his wife because she talked too much. When the senator asked the man what his wife talked about, he replied, "She don't say."[10]

One of Sam P. Jones' contemporaries called him a "running fire of fun." This witness, who succeeded Jones in his first circuit, said: "Every man, woman and child was made the subject of his humor. He saw something ridiculous in every situation. From the time he entered a home until he left it, the whole house was kept in an uproar. No one could escape the lightning flashes of his kindly wit."[11]

Jesus apparently used humor in dealing with the Syrophoenician woman (see Mark 7:24-30). She was a stranger to him, yet he bantered with her. Paul's word, "Let your speech . . . be . . . seasoned with salt" (Col. 4:6) may also be a reference to the use of humor in witnessing.

I agree with the person who said, "God must have a sense of humor because he called me into his service." A Godlike sense of humor will surely help us to communicate his word to strangers.

Conclusion

We began our look at the stranger barrier by reading from the Book of Ruth. Ruth was not only a stranger to Naomi at first; she was a Moabite. Why did Ruth claim her mother-in-law's God? Could it have been due to Naomi's godly life-style? Sometime we can overcome the stranger barrier through our Christian life-style.

Two things at least remain to be said about breaking down this objection. First, we can with confidence affirm the possibility of winning total strangers to Christ. Moreover, it is also possible for God's servants to serve strangers in future generations. We can do that through our influence upon our children, our children's children, and our friends' children and grandchildren. We can serve future generations through our faithful stewardship of exhaustible resources. We can also serve the future generations through our works of art and literature. And perhaps most of all we can influence strangers in the future through our faithful stewardship of the gospel today.

Second, we need to say again what Jesus and Paul said. "Others have labored, and you have entered into their labor" (John 4:38). One plants, another waters, but God gives the increase (see 1 Cor. 3:5-9). God has other agents at work for him too! You may not be the *only* (and probably not even the first) witness to teach this prospect something about God. Don't be so self-righteous as to believe like Elijah that you are the only faithful one left. God still has his "7,000" who have not bowed their knee to Baal.

Notes

1. Tim Nicholas, *More Than Just Talk* (Atlanta: Home Mission Board, SBC, 1977), p. 156.

2. Judy Foreman, "Friend Also May Be Lifesaver, Social Scientists Say," *The News and Observer*, 25 Mar. 1982, p. 21A.

3. See the AP report, "Professional Listeners Hear It All," *The News and Observer*, 1981 Dec. 6, p. 7-III.

4. John F. Havlik, "Back to the Bible?" *Missions USA*, 53, No. 2, (Mar.-Apr. 1982), p. 52.

5. Eugene Skelton, *A Walk in the Light* (Richmond: Skipworth Press, Inc., 1980), pp. 49-50.

6. Ibid., p. 65.

7. Related by Laura Fry Allen to a meeting of SBC evangelism leaders in the fall of 1981 at Nashville, Tennessee. I am indebted to Mrs. Allen for a rough draft of the story and a letter authenticating it dated Dec. 15, 1981. Mrs. Allen has changed the names and place to protect the identity of those involved.

8. See "Ministry: Sharing the Gospel in Practical Ways," *Baptist Courier*, 114, No. 17, 29 Apr. 1982, p. 14.

9. See the Baptist Press release, "SBTS Student Turns Hatred into Ministry," *Word and Way*, 119, No. 1, 7 Jan. 1982, p. 7.

10. See Linda Brown, "Humor Is Serious Matter, Sam Ervin Tells Group," *The News and Observer*, 21 Nov. 1981, p. 25.

11. Mrs. Sam P. Jones and Walt Holcomb, *The Life and Sayings of Sam P. Jones*, 2nd rev. ed. (Atlanta: The Franklin-Turner Co., 1907, pp. 71-72.

11
The Age Barrier

Objection: "I'm too old."

Scripture Lesson: Deuteronomy 34:7; Titus 2:2-6

Introduction

Clara was saved at age eight. She was in her living room. Her older sister was playing and singing "My Faith Looks Up to Thee." Immediately she leapt up and ran to tell her mother. She didn't know then that a Christian was supposed to share her faith. But she did spontaneously. Later, Clara discovered that she should share her faith. She was eighteen when she started doing it intentionally. She is now nearly eighty, but she's still looking persons in the eyes and telling them about Jesus.

Yet some Christians when asked to share their faith say, "I'm too old." There are those who apparently believe that at a certain point senior citizens in the kingdom of God get too old to propagate the Christian faith.

On Being Too Young

More often have I heard the objection of being too old than that of being too young. The age barrier is no respecter of persons. It applies both to the old and the young. That may indeed be a manifest weakness in this objection. Those who say, "I'm too old," raise no more valid an objection than those who say, "I'm too young."

The renowned Jonathan Edwards, under whom the great awakening began in America, related in much detail how four-year-old Phebe Bartlet was influenced toward Christ by the witness of her eleven-year-old brother. Then, this settled and mature pastor described the continuing witness of little Phebe to her older sisters.

I have no doubt but that Edwards intended this example as a

model illustrating the kind of religious affections which the revival in Northampton stirred up. Edwards went to considerable length to show that the very young were capable of strong religious affections, and were also able to bear a credible Christian witness to others.[1]

My conjecture is that since there is no comparable example of the very old being saved and bearing witness to the unsaved in Edwards' *Faithful Narrative,* eighteenth century Christians in America more frequently raised the objection of "I'm too young" than of "I'm too old." Today, the situation is exactly the opposite in this last quarter of the twentieth century.

There can be little doubt that more persons are saved at a younger than at an older age in our country. One pastor, for example, surveyed 253 believers to determine what age group was most receptive to the gospel. Here is what he found:

Under 20 years	138 were saved
Between 20 and 30	85 were saved
Between 30 and 40	22 were saved
Between 40 and 50	4 were saved
Between 50 and 60	3 were saved
Between 60 and 70	1 was saved[2]

Nevertheless, it does not automatically follow that older persons cannot be saved. More important still, there is nothing in the statistics which would indicate that older Christians cannot lead lost persons to faith in Christ.

Modern Examples

On the contrary, consider several modern examples of older Christians who have either remained or become active in evangelism. C. E. Autrey, the former director of evangelism for Southern Baptists, at seventy-five years of age is still going strong for Christ in Salt Lake City, Utah. He pastors University Baptist Church, directs Seminary Center, works with the Baptist Student Union, and teaches part-time at Brigham Young University. Each month Autrey averages 400 visits or contacts for the church. He doesn't like to be introduced as the *former* director of evangelism for the Home Mission Board or *former* anything. "I want to tell what I'm doing *now,"* said Autrey. "I'm not on a shelf, gathering dust. I may be *kicking* up a little dust, though."[3]

Gonzalo Báez-Camargo, whom *Christianity Today* called "Mexico's Grand Old Man of Evangelism," said when he was eighty-one years old: "My day lasts generally from 7 or 8 a.m. to 9 p.m. . . . Being active makes you feel very useful. It gives you the feeling that you have not been put aside. That feeling kills people. It's an oppressive condition that shortens life."[4]

D. A. McGavran, the father of the modern church growth movement, was fifty-seven years old when his first seminal book *The Bridges of God* was published. He was sixty-three when he became the founding dean of the School of World Mission at Fuller Theological Seminary in Pasadena, California. He was sixty-six when he started publishing his *Global Church Growth Bulletin.* He was seventy-two when his foundational book *Understanding Church Growth* was first published. McGavran has continued to speak, teach, and write into his eighties.

Two missionaries resigned in 1974 after serving fourteen hectic years in eastern Africa. That couple looked forward to a long, quiet ministry in the United States prior to their retirement. But in 1982, when the man was fifty-five years of age, they left their children and grandchildren and returned to spend at least ten more years as evangelistic missionaries in Kenya.[5] We don't get too old to serve God, not even in cross-cultural evangelism—to say nothing of monocultural evangelism.

Bill Harrill, one of my former students, was introduced to Christ by a young man around thirty. When the young man approached Harrill, Harrill said, "I'm too old." At that time he was fifty-six. Not only did Harrill discover he was not too old to be saved, but he found out that he was not too old to serve God and to try to get other persons saved. He enrolled in seminary one week before his fifty-ninth birthday. His fellow students called him "The Golden Seminarian."[6]

It's never too late to start doing the will of God. I have taught two men in their sunset years. One man was in his eighties working on a second doctorate. Another was in his seventies and had retired from public school administration.

I was in a meeting of lay Christians one Friday night. We were at a conference center. It was an "after-service" gathering for singing and spontaneous testifying. An elderly lady with gray hair stood up and said, "Praise God you never get too old to share your faith." I wholeheartedly agree. An elderly Christian can even still introduce a young person to Jesus. This is cross-generational witnessing.

Never Too Old

Don't ever think you are too old to do things that matter for yourself and for others. Eighty-six-year-old Quirl Thompson Havenhill of New Mexico repairs her own car, a 1939 Dodge. She built her own house with her own hands at age sixty-five. She makes some of the best and most beautiful quilts in the whole country. She grows most of her own food. She does not pollute the good earth with garbage to be hauled off by some garbage man.

Why is Quirl, as she is affectionately called, so good at what she does? "If you make careful plans, it'll come out right," she says. "Everything has a time. And everything has a right way to be done. Lay it out. Plan it out. And it'll be right for you. I like to dream on things that is (sic.) maybe just possible. But I always do better when I choose out of them (sic.) possibles what's the most probable."[7]

The Bible says, "Where there is no vision, the people perish" (Prov. 29:18a, KJV). So long as older Christians have a vision of lost people being saved, they are dreaming a possible dream. Like Quirl, they can be good and effective if they will plan their witnessing and choose the most probable from among the possibles.

Julia Dillingham invented a useful device called Fill and Freeze when she was about eighty years of age. At age eighty-one she said, "I have confidence in myself. There is not a thing in my mind that I want to do that I'm afraid to try."[8] Older Christians who have confidence in themselves and faith in God will likewise not be afraid to try any legitimate method of faith sharing.

Here is another true story. Walt Fredericks was fifty-seven years old and, by his own admission, fat. He couldn't get out of his bathtub! Fredericks went to his doctor, thinking it was too late for him to begin a preventive maintenance program on his body. His doctor assured him it was not too late and put him on a strict walking program. Eventually he became a jogger. At age sixty-two Walt Fredericks successfully ran the Boston Marathon. At age seventy he was still running and throwing the javelin.[9] It's seldom too late to start getting one's body in shape. It's never too late for Christians to start getting the souls of their fellow human beings in shape for time and eternity.

The age barrier is often an illusion. It may be applied to both the very young and the very old, and all the way in-between. Like Melchizedek it is without beginning of days or ending of days. Gail Sheehy, for example, found that working-class men think of themselves as middle-aged at forty and old by sixty. By contrast, business executives and professionals see themselves as not reaching middle age until fifty and old age at seventy.[10]

Modern examples of older Christians who have remained or become active in witnessing abound. If these living senior Christians can share their faith, you can too. You are never too old to bear witness to Jesus Christ. An evangelist died in 1976 at the age of 122. He had been active in his evangelistic career up to two weeks before his death. "The Lord didn't give me no time to retire," said that longtime evangelist in the last year of his life.[11]

Retirees in Name Only

Louis Harris and Associates did a 1982 study for the National Council of Aging entitled "Aging in the Eighties: America in Transition." The study found that most retirees do not want to sit idle. Americans are retiring in name only.[12]

Louis Pell of New York is one example which gives flesh and blood to that Harris study. Pell tried to retire at seventy-two from his own successful plumbing business. "That lasted six weeks," said Pell. "I walked myself to death. I couldn't sleep. I didn't eat good." Finally, he told his wife he was going back to work. Her reply was, "You're too old." But Pell did get a job, and that was thirteen years ago. At eighty-five he was still working. Pell said: "I see these sixty-five-year-old guys on Social Security hanging around and fading away. They're killing themselves doing nothing."[13]

Contrary to some popular stereotypes, only 5 percent of those

Americans sixty-five and over live in institutions of any kind. Of the remaining 95 percent, only 14 or 15 percent of them are in need of constant companionship. That leaves 80 percent of them still active or able to be active.[14]

Some of these retirees are going back to school. A ninety-two-year-old Utah woman with children, grandchildren, great grand-children, and great-great grandchildren graduated from high school in 1982. Her son, who was Utah's superintendent of public instruction, retired from his post in July of 1982.[15]

An Ohio man returend to college at age ninety-three. When they asked him why he was back in college at that age, he replied: "It's a good way to spend my time."[16] Senior citizens do have time on their hands—lots of it. What better way to use that time than to bear a witness to Jesus Christ?

Senior citizens often have valuable skills. Joseph Mazer, who celebrated his one hundredth birthday in 1974 was by turns a diamond cutter, watchmaker, optometrist, attorney, and jeweler.[17] If we overlook the vast array of skills which retirees have, we shall neglect a potential gold mine of talents, ability, and experience—much of which may be enlisted in the service of witnessing.

Some senior adults also still have an abundance of physical strength. Think of Zachariah D. Blackistone, a Washington, D.C. florist. Blackistone once sold flowers to Teddy Roosevelt. When he celebrated his 103rd birthday, he was still actively involved in his floral business, working every day. More surprisingly this 103-year-old still jogs 200 yards each morning before leaving for work.[18] Any senior citizen with that much energy has the necessary physical and mental powers to be an effective witness to that good news which the Bible calls the dynamite of God (see Rom. 1:16).

Consider also Larry Lewis who died at 106 in San Francisco. Lewis, a former circus aerialist and assistant to the great escape artist Houdini, was a veritable dynamo. He could outrun and out-walk men half his age. This centenarian ran 6.7 miles each day in Golden Gate Park. He could run 100 yards in just over seventeen seconds, and boxed every day at the Olympic Club. Lewis celebrated his 102nd birthday by running 100 yards in 17.3 seconds. "Anybody can do what I've done," said Lewis. "Nobody is too old, either."[19] I am not sure that just anybody could do what Lewis did, but I do believe that we should tap the great reservoir of strength which remains in Christian senior citizens and use that energy to share Christ with the unreconciled.

Worldwide by 1985, it is estimated that there will be 270 million men and women who have reached the age of sixty-five or over. In some developed nations senior adults will make up 20 percent or more of the population.[20]

The fastest growing age group in America is senior adults. By the year 2000, they will constitute 20 percent of our population. Presently, they are in excess of 11 percent. In 1900, only 3 percent of Americans were sixty-five and over.[21]

It may startle some of us to learn that there were 9,400 centenarians in the United States in 1977 and about 19,000 in the Soviet Union. Some Russian scientists have even expressed the belief that persons can live to be 400 years old or more.[22]

Christians who are senior citizens will come closer to reaching lost adults in that same age group than anyone else. If the church is to keep pace with this rapid growth of world citizens aged sixty-five and over, we shall have to mobilize the senior citizens of the kingdom of God to witness with greater intentionality to their lost peers.

The Attitudinal Factor

Swift may have been correct when he observed that no wise man ever wished to be younger. That is the reason columnist George F. Will wrote when he turned forty: "It is said that God gave us memory so we could have roses in winter. But it is also true that without memory we could not have a self in any season. The more memories you have, the more 'you' you have."[23]

Attitude has a great deal to do with overcoming the age barrier to witnessing. Persons grow old by deserting their ideals. Years may wrinkle our skin, but the loss of interest can wrinkle our soul. General Douglas MacArthur voiced my sentiments when he said: "You are as young as your faith, as old as your doubt, as young as your self-confidence, as old as your fear, as young as your hope, as old as your despair."

Investigators at Duke University's Center for the Study of Aging and Human Development found a close correlation between persons' psychological attitudes and how well they fare in later years. A high "happiness" rating, they found, coincided with a longer life. This is not to deny the influence of diet, drugs, or the manipulation of genes. Rather, it is to affirm that remaining active in some meaningful social role affects people's longevity on the physical, psychological and social levels.[24]

I am hard pressed to think of any more meaningful social or religious role one can fill than that of helping persons find meaning, purpose, and fulfillment in Jesus Christ and his church.

Some persons view the world as a giant garbage dump while others see it as God's cathedral. Meditate a few moments on this modern parable: Grandma came home from church dressed in her Sunday best. But she stepped out of her car carrying a large, green trash bag buldging with empty beer cans, bottles, and sandwich wrappers. "What in the world are you doing?" gulped her granddaughter. "Cleaning up the lane," said Grandma matter-of-factly. "I do it every Sunday after church." When her granddaughter looked even more bewildered, she explained: "To me the world is God's cathedral, darling. I'm just tidying my pew."[25] That attitude which we prize most highly among Kingdom witnesses is epitomized in the person who is always tidying up her pew in God's cathedral.

Conclusion

Perhaps the aging which we need to guard against most diligently is a religious aberration and mutation of progeria. Progeria, as you probably know, is a rare aging disease which turns an eight-year-old child physiologically into an eighty-year-old person. It ages its victims ten times faster than normal, stunts growth, and often results in death by the teen years.

Three victims of progeria made the front pages of US newspapers in 1981. What a sight! Eight-and nine-year-olds baldheaded, wearing caps, arthritic, and looking as though they were eighty or ninety years old.

One surprise in it all was that each of the three, two boys and one girl, was thought by his or her respective families to be the only one suffering from the disease. The two boys met in Disneyland and became fast friends as they discovered their cherished fairy-tale world.[26]

Wouldn't it be super if a place like Disneyland were the real world? Alas! The real world is Orkney, South Africa, and Hallsville, Texas. Progeria is one of those painful realities which some of God's image bearers must endure.

Those who say, "I'm too old to witness," may be affected with a type of religious progeria. But unlike physical progeria, there is a cure for religious progeria. Jesus Christ is the only real fountain of youth (see John 10:10).

The psalmist ties old age and the presence of God to the proclamation of God's wondrous deeds:

> Do not cast me off in the time of old
>   age;
> forsake me not when my strength is
>   spent . . .
> O God, from my youth thou hast
>   taught me,
> and I still proclaim thy wondrous
>   deeds.
> So even to old age and gray hairs,
>   O God, do not forsake me,
> till I proclaim thy might
>   to all generations to come (Ps. 71:9, 17-18).

Finally, if we think of age fifty as the golden anniversary of one's life, then perhaps all the years following age fifty may be called our golden years. A. T. Robertson conjectures that Paul was about fifty years of age when he began his evangelistic ministry and sixty-five when it ended.[27] Whether we are fifty, sixty-five, eighty, or whatever age, we need to ponder how one professor at Georgetown College in Kentucky used to set his hourglass on the desk. As the sand poured quickly from top to bottom, he would say: "What you are going to do you'd better do quickly."

Notes

1. Jonathan Edwards, "The Great Awakening," *The Works of Jonathan Edwards,* Vol. 4, ed. C. C. Goen (New Haven: Yale University Press, 1972), pp. 199-205.

2. Viola Walden, *The Sword of the Lord,* LXVIII, No. 4, 22 Jan. 1982, p. 4.

3. Mike Creswell, "Kicking Up Dust," *Missions USA,* 53, No. 2 (Mar.-Apr. 1982), pp. 64-69.

4. See the interview by John Maust, "An Interview with Gonzalo Báez-Camargo: Mexico's Grand Old Man of Evangelism," *Christianity Today,* XXVI, No. 5, 5 Mar. 1982, p. 31.

5. See "Two Missouri 'Old Folks' Heading Back to Missions," *Word and Way,* 119, No. 1, 7 Jan. 1982, p. 4.

6. This is the true testimony of William Davis Harrill of Forest City, NC. I am using it with his permission and encouragement.

7. See Norma Bradly Allen, "Quirl's Way," *Woman's Day,* 3 Nov. 1981, pp. 44-46, 144.

8. Dennis Rogers, "Inventor's Tragic Past Yields to New Life," *The News and Observer,* 16 Feb. 1982, p. Cl.

9. Told by Robert H. Schuller in a sermon entitled "Follow Your Guiding Star" in 1978 at Garden Grove Community Church, Garden Grove, CA.

10. Cited from an excerpt of Gail Sheehy's *Passages* in *Delta Airline Magazine,* Oct. 1976, p. 56.

11. See the AP report, "Evangelist Dies at Age 122," *The State,* 26 May 1976, p. 5-D.

12. See "Americans Retiring in Name Only," *The News and Observer,* 31 May 1982, p. 8A.

13. See "Work at 85 One Man's Answer," *The Sun,* 24 July 1973, p. B-3.

14. See the interview by Toby Druin with Tom Prevost, "To Rage Against the Dying of the Light," *Home Missions,* 47, No. 3 (Mar. 1976), pp. 27-32.

15. Reported in *Anderson Independent-Mail,* 30 May 1982, p. 2A.

16. See the AP report, "Ohio Man Returns to College at Age 93," *The State,* 12 Mar. 1976, p. 15-A.

17. See the AP report, "100-Year-Old Truly 'Jack of All Trades,'" *The State,* 15 Aug. 1974, p. 18-C.

18. Reported in *The Charlotte Observer,* 16 Feb. 1974, p. 22B.

19. See the UPI report, "Former Circus Acrobat Larry Lewis, 106, Dies," *The State,* 3 Feb. 1974, p. 16A.

20. Margaret H. and S. Allen Bacon, "Time to Retire?" *The Christian Century,* XC, No. 7, 14 Feb. 1973, p. 201.

21. Druin, "To Rage Against the Dying of the Light," *Home Missions,* p. 27.

22. Dan Fisher, "Soviet Researchers Foresee Methuselah's Children," *The State,* 14 Aug. 1977, p. 5-B.

23. George F. Will, "On Turning 40," *Newsweek,* 27 Apr. 1981, p. 104.

24. See "Can Aging Be Cured?" *Newsweek,* 16 Apr. 1973, pp. 57-66.

25. Adapted from *Guideposts* as quoted by the *Sprouts* edition of *Seeds,* Sept. 1981, p. 6.

26. See the AP report, "Fransie, Mickey Meet Their Cherished Fairy-Tale Heroes," *The Tennesseean,* 3 Dec. 1981, p. 11.

27. A. T. Robertson, *Epochs in the Life of Paul* (Nashville: Broadman Press, 1976), p. 11.

12
The Kinship-Friendship Barrier

Objection: "I'm too close."

Scripture Lesson: The Song of Solomon 1:6*b*; 1 Peter 3:1-6

Introduction

Nancy L. McAvoy became a Christian at the Billy Graham crusade in Portland, Oregon in 1968. Her conversion was the first in a long line. One year later her son, Marc, and her daughter, Callie, aged eight and seven respectively, confessed faith in Christ during nightly devotions. Following that, her alcoholic husband was saved in a home Bible study.

Shortly thereafter, the McAvoy family gave themselves to Christ. Later, Nancy's own brother and his family came to Christ. Then, her husband's brother, who was in prison, became a Christian. Finally, her youngest son, Danny, accepted Christ.

Now McAvoy's husband is completing his doctorate in theology, preparing himself to teach Bible in college or seminary.[1] That is the kind of chain reaction we seek and frequently see in true evangelism. One person's conversion can lead to the salvation of a whole family or of an extended family.

Nevertheless, there are some among us who believe and teach that we are too close to our own family and friends to lead them to Christ. When I returned home from the Korean conflict in 1951 and started to college the next year, I was burdened for the salvation of some of my kinfolk and friends. Some well-meaning Christians convinced me that I was too close to them, and that someone else would be more likely to introduce these dear ones to the Lord.

I had begun to feel comfortable in saying "I'm too close" until subsequent events convinced me that I was the most likely person in all the world to influence my own lost loved ones toward Christ.

Especially is that true if you are a first-generation Christian, that is, the first person in your family to become a believer in Christ.

The Closer, the Better

This idea that we are too close to kin and friends to share our faith with them has begun to change to exactly its opposite. Some are now vigorously contending that our deepest relationships are our best witnessing opportunities.[2]

I am personally pricked by that word of Scripture: "they made me keeper of the vineyards; but, my own vineyard I have not kept!" (Song of Sol. 1:6b). How sad and even tragic it would be for us to compass land and sea making disciples of strangers, but all the while neglect to share our most precious treasure with those nearest and dearest to our hearts.

The closer we are to lost individuals, the better are our chances of winning them to the Lord. Also, the evidence is beginning to mount that the closer we are to those whom we win, the greater likelihood there is that they will become active and responsible members of the church. One study found that when a new convert saw the person who led him or her to Christ as a friend, there was a 71 percent chance that the convert would become an active and responsible church member. However, when the new convert saw the church member as a salesperson, there was an 85 percent chance that he or she would drop out within the first six months.[3]

Flavil R. Yeakley, Jr., reported on research which shows the importance of friendship in the process of becoming a new disciple. The study identified 240 new Christians presently active and involved in their churches. In addition, a second group of 240 people were identified who could be classified as "dropouts." (They had made a recent decision but had since lapsed into inactivity.) A third group of 240 people were identified who had been presented with the gospel message but had chosen not to make a positive decision.

In individual interviews with these 720 people, each was asked to classify the person who had presented the gospel into one of three categories: "Friend," "Salesperson," or "Teacher." The results provided some startling conclusions: the people who saw the church member as a "friend" were almost all now Christians and active in their churches (94 percent). On the other hand, those people who saw the church member as a "salesperson" often made an initial decision but soon dropped out in large numbers (71 percent later dropped out). Finally, those who saw the church member as a "teacher" generally tended to not respond at all (84 percent said "no thanks").

The implications are clear. The non-Christian person who perceives your relationship as one of a "friend" is far more likely to eventually respond to Christ's love than the person who sees you either as a "teacher"—instructing on doctrine, sin, and morality or as a "salesperson"—manipulating toward an eventual decision.[4]

That witness who is more concerned with collecting scalps than with making disciples is engaged in what I call "cowboy-and-Indian" evangelism. The evangelist who is itching to add another notch to his evangelism gun rather than add another name to the Lamb's book of life is also playing "cowboy-and-Indian" evangelism.

Some lone rangers may have been quite useful in bringing law and order to America's wild West. But lone ranger-type evangelists, who are not themselves tied to a local church and who do not diligently seek to tie their converts to some local church, are what Paul calls "peddlers of God's word" (2 Cor. 2:17).

We Christians are royalty, and we ought to act like Christ our King rather than like hucksters. Isn't there a myth about a frog being kissed and turning into a handsome prince? Conversion is the process of turning frogs into princesses and princes. God kisses us with the love of his Son and transforms us into our true selves. Unregenerated persons are under a spell as it were. They have a curse upon them. They are not what their Creator intended them to become. Genuine conversion is that process which returns us to our original, royal status. We Christians are all princes and princesses of God. We are a Kingdom of priests who reign with God over his creation.

Evangelism ought to be an ethical enterprise. At its best, it is an engagement between friends, a relational and dialogical confrontation where the truth is spoken in love. Sensitive persuasion is most convincing when it takes place in the context of a Christian presence and a faithful proclamation of the reign of God.

God's Bridges

One sure way to overcome the kinship-friendship barrier is to see kinship and friendship as the natural bridges of God. The natural webs of kinship, friendship, and association are the bridges across which God often chooses to move into the lives of people everywhere. If we would share the gospel with a trumpet sound, let us note that the loudest and clearest trumpets God provides us are our deepest relationships with one another.

Here is a fantastic story of how God worked through the life and witness of one man—Henry Bilbrey. He became a Christian in October 1979 at the age of thirty-seven. Jesus Christ revolutionized Bilbrey's life. He had been an introvert, indifferent to others. He was a shift worker in a large manufacturing plant.

Following his conversion this new Christian led seventeen of his neighbors and friends to faith in Christ and four others to join the church by transfer of membership. Bilbrey seized every available moment to witness to others. He began as early as six in the morning and continued until late in the night. Five-and-a-half months after his conversion, he died of a sudden heart attack.

Two men to whom Bilbrey had witnessed became Christians at his funeral. The next Sunday two more persons confessed faith in Christ. It is said by those who knew him that Bilbrey literally won his whole street to Christ.

His influence was so powerful that even though he was dead he continued to speak. Within one month following Bilbrey's death, thirty persons had come into the church as a result of his continuing influence. They found two of his notebooks which contained the names of thirty-six persons for whom he had been praying, some of whom he had visited. Friends and neighbors with whom he had worked expressed a desire to continue his ministry with those thirty-six prospects.[5] That thrilling story is not yet finished and will not be until all accounts are settled in the judgment by God himself.

The same God who walked into the lives of so many persons through the life and witness of Henry Bilbrey wants to move through you and me into the lives of our lost friends, neighbors, and family members. "The most effective witness," wrote Rosalind Rinker, "is that natural witness of friends who have found the Way themselves. Friends who talk calmly, sincerely, and even casually of Christ, and the difference He makes in their lives."[6]

"Glorious, fervent friendships are still the best way of reaching youth," said A. C. Archibald. "Friendship ruins many of them; it can also save them."[7] Increasingly, we are finding out that the same statements apply to adults.

If we don't have any lost friends, we ought to make some. "If a man does not make new acquaintances as he advances through life," Samuel Johnson cautioned in 1775, "he will soon find himself left alone. A man . . . should keep his friendships in constant repair."[8] Doubly should the Christian who would witness with intentionality heed the advice of that saintly and intellectual giant.

David Adeney says of the church in China: "The most basic form of evangelism is through personal friendships in which the gospel is shared with relatives and neighbors." Adeney also believes that the testimony of answered prayer, especially in healing the sick, has led many to faith in Christ.[9]

Those nearest us usually can hurt or help us the most. That was true of Jesus' family. "If every person in the world knew what everybody else said about the other," said Pascal, "there would not be four friends left in the world." Friendship is something at which we really have to work. The two words *turf* and *trust* are important in communicating even among friends.

Knowledge sometimes gets in the way of knowledge in witnessing. It may even be pitted against knowledge. It was hard for the woman of Samaria in John 4 to know who Jesus was because she knew something else about Jesus. Similarly, it may be hard for us to know a particular black person because we know blacks, to know a particular Korean because we know Koreans, or to know a particular friend because we know friends, etc. I suspect that some of our knowledge of our friends and family members is often pitted against other knowledge of them, and this is one reason some of us have difficulty seeing kinship and friendship as the bridges of God. Our unpleasant knowledge of them, so to speak, serves as a mental block to screen out the more pleasant knowledge.

The Greek text of John 4:9 makes it clear that Jews had no

friendly dealings with Samaritans. You have to have dealings with others even if you don't like them. If our relationships with family, friends, and fellow workers are the natural bridges for the traffic of the gospel, we ought to diligently strive to establish friendly dealings with them.

God's Timing

Rinker makes something of following God's timing in witnessing to friends. We can find God's timing through the art of listening, asking questions, and making provocative statements, thinks Rinker.[10]

Can you see God's timing through the art of listening in the following incident? A member of First Baptist Church, Moore, Oklahoma, was hurrying to finish a job at her work so she could get to the Tuesday night school of evangelism. One of her co-workers inquired of her why she was in such a hurry. She explained that she was learning to share her faith so she could go tell people about the Lord. The lady responded, "You need to share it around here."

That hit home, so later the church member waited around at the time clock to ask her if she was serious. When she responded positively, this evangelistic trainee took her aside privately and led her to Christ. The following Sunday night, the new convert made her public profession of faith.[11]

A favorite pastime for many Americans is playing the game "Ain't It Awful?" Griping is another name for it. We sit or stand around talking about how awful is the weather or the economy or the working conditions, etc. When our friends and family members play "Ain't It Awful," that may be an appropriate time for the provocative statement: "You talk like God is dead!"

Behind that statement are many things you have learned. You are giving your friends something to think about. God is alive, and his presence makes a difference.[12] Such a statement, properly timed and toned, may gain you the opening you seek to tell of the hope which is within you.

God's timing is geared to the needs of individuals and families. Nicodemus came to Jesus out of a deep sense of felt need (see John 3:1-15). The official whose son was ill desperately wanted to see his son healed (see John 4:46-54). Jesus sought to meet the real needs of actual persons in the first century. We are not likely to be far from God's timing if we copy Jesus in that respect.

Jean's fiancé was killed in an automobile accident. She was living in a nurses' dormitory. Most of the girls whispered and tiptoed as they passed Jean's door. Jean was packing her clothes and getting ready to attend the funeral.

Mary couldn't go past that door without identifying with Jean in some small way. She knocked. "All I could say to her," said Mary afterwards, "was that I understood because I'd lost my father not long before." Also, Mary had said: "I know there isn't too much I can do to help, but I know One who can. Try praying to him. That helped me when I couldn't stand it."

Jean at once sought out Mary when she got back from the funeral. "You were the only girl in the whole dorm that came to my room after I got the telegram," said Jean. "I want to know you better. You were kind to me. I did pray, and it helped."

Out of that friendship Mary shared the gospel with Jean, and Jean became a follower of the One who has promised one day to wipe away all of our tears.[13] If we likewise will follow God's timing in meeting the needs of our friends and loved ones, we can overcome the kinship-friendship barrier in our faith sharing. *Agape* love is something we do.

Conclusion

Three more things need to be said. First, my experience and observation have taught me several additional suggestions which I offer for breaking down the kinship-friendship barrier:

- Pick up on their interest or a point of identification. These are touching points.
- Always be open to others.
- It takes time, so don't give up.
- Pray for them daily.
- Let them know you really care. That's *agapē*.
- Visit new people in the community.
- Let them know you are human also.
- Use the doors God opens to you at work.

Second, when I raise the objection "I'm too close," that may reveal the need for a more radical change and greater Christlikeness in my own life. What it may tell me is that I need a better walk with Christ, so my walk will more closely match my talk.

Third, meditate on this story and be guided by it: Years ago in England, there lived a fine preacher named John Holden. One late afternoon in the village where he lived, everyone began to run to the seashore to man rowboats to go out into the sea where a vessel had capsized. Little boat after little boat would go out and bring to shore those who had been thrown into the icy waters.

When the last rowboat was coming in, John Holden standing on shore called out to the rowboat, "Did you get the last one?"

Came the reply from the little boat, "I think there's one more, but I can't find him."

John Holden began immediately to prepare to go out in his own little boat. His mother grabbed him and said, "Oh son, it's so dark and foggy—don't go out there. You may never come back."

John Holden said, "Mother, I love you, but I've got to go out there."

After what seemed to be an interminable time, John Holden's little rowboat could be seen through the night and fog. Someone on shore shouted out, "Did you get him? Was there one more out there? Did you get him?"

"Yes, I got him and tell my mother, it's my brother."[14]

Notes

1. Nancy L. McAvoy, "The Story of Nancy L. McAvoy," *Decision*, 23, Nos. 8-9 (July-Aug. 1982), p. 14.

2. See, for example, W. Oscar Thompson, Jr., *Concentric Circles of Concern* (Nashville: Broadman Press, 1981); Ron Johnson, Joseph W. Hinkle, Charles M. Lowry, *Oikos: A Practical Approach to Family Evangelism* (Nashville: Broadman Press, 1982).

3. Alan Loy McGinnis, rev. of *The Friendship Factor Church Growth: America*, 8, No. 1 (Jan.-Feb. 1982) 18.

4. Flavil R. Yeakley, Jr., "Research for the Growing Church," *Church Growth: America*, 7, No. 1 (Jan.-Feb. 1981), p. 10.

5. Related by Frank Crumpler in a printed booklet, *Churches Alive and Grow-*

ing, p. 14, n.d., published by the Evangelism Section of the Home Mission Board, SBC, Atlanta, Georgia.

6. Rosalind Rinker, *You Can Witness with Confidence* (Grand Rapids: Zondervan Publishing House, 1962), p. 72.

7. Arthur C. Archibald, *New Testament Evangelism* (Philadelphia: The Judson Press, 1946), p. 133.

8. Judy Foreman, "Friend Also May Be Lifesaver, Social Scientists Say," *The News and Observer*, 25 Mar. 1982, p. 21A.

9. David Adeney, "Springtime for the Church in China," *Christianity Today*, XXVI, No. 11, 18 June 1982, p. 30.

10. Rinker, *You Can Witness*, p. 71.

11. Related in the First Baptist Church, Moore, Oklahaoma, edition of *The Baptist Messenger*, 70, No. 37, 17 Sept. 1981, p. 16.

12. See Rinker, *You Can Witness*, pp. 71-72.

13. Ibid., p. 73. I have slightly revised the story and retold it in my own terminology.

14. Related by Bailey E. Smith in his president's address to the 1981 meeting of the SBC. See *The Word and Way*, 118, No. 24, 11 June 1981, p. 4.